I0818902

ianka fleerackers

OWN YOUR STORY

or someone else will

Lannoo
Campus

This book was originally published in Dutch as *Own your story. Or someone else will*. Personal branding en thought leadership voor professionals met een reputatie, LannooCampus, 2023.

D/2024/45/361 – ISBN 9789401445221– NUR 808

Interior design: Wendy De Haes
Cover design: Karl Demoen

LannooCampus Publishers is a subsidiary of Lannoo Publishers, the book and multimedia division of Lannoo Publishers nv.

LannooCampus Publishers
Vaartkom 41 box 01.02
3000 Leuven
Belgium
www.lannoocampus.com

P.O. Box 23202
1100 DS Amsterdam
The Netherlands

Contents

PROLOGUE: IT'S UP TO YOU

Everywhere in the world, people follow people because of who they are, the stories they tell, the changes they initiate in their environment or in the world at large. We encounter them through the internet, traditional media, products, and services. We see them in videos, read their content, listen to their speeches, and become captivated by their influence. They are referred to as influencers, personal brands, celebrities, leaders, and thought leaders. Thanks to technology and social media, anyone now can become influential. There seem to be so many already that the internet appears to be oversaturated with individuals keen to showcase themselves, show their best side, and make you believe that you need them. If this makes you feel disheartened, or disinclined to try yourself, then I understand. I too struggle with not wanting to further fill an already brimming bucket with my own contributions. But if you truly believe in your heart that you have something of value to offer and you choose not to because of this, you're only setting yourself up for frustration, to ultimately become a grumpy old person, bitterly counting down your days in a retirement home.

I've written this book for two reasons: the first is to inspire you, and the second, to give you insight. I aim to inspire you to lead, to step into the limelight and share your story with your tribe. To lead a life where you don't need to conform to a label that's been slapped onto you, where you aren't too much of this or that. There are people in the world who are meant to follow, and there are those meant to lead. And although it might seem nowadays that it's better to be a leader and that everyone is a leader, that's not true. And that's all right. We need both. This book can help you uncover in what ways and to what extent you can be a leader. I also want to offer insight, yet this book is not a how-to guide. I won't teach you how to defeat the algorithm of LinkedIn, nor provide the best tips for creating a video. A book is no longer the appropriate format for that; besides, it would be outdated within six months.

I have a different plan for you. With this book, I want to provoke you to think about how you wish to utilise personal branding in your life: not solely as a marketing strategy but as a means to build a legacy.

I write this book with a background in arts and media and a passion for art and literature. My career as an actress meant that in traditional media, I was a recognised celebrity. Today, I am predominantly visible online, perform on stage as 'myself', and continue to build my brand there. This provides an additional layer of experience, which I know many involved in personal branding and public speaking coaching lack. In the best cases, they have worked behind the scenes in a media company, but never in front of the camera, they haven't been subject to tabloid gossip, or had to deal with criticism in the press. Even more so, many are only familiar with social media as the means to build a personal brand and are just now making their first steps onto the stage or as an author. In this, I wish to make a difference. I've done it all. And no, it's not arrogance or conceit. It is simply a fact. My experience also means that my perspective on professional personal branding is different. To me, personal branding isn't just an online phenomenon; it's not an ego story, and not about fame.

This book is for you, the professional with an established reputation, a track record of ten years or more, and an intellectual frustration: you have more to say than what you are currently doing. You could be an employee, part of the C-level suite of a company, wanting to amplify your voice within or outside your job. You could be a CEO aspiring to thought leadership. Or you might be a solo entrepreneur seeking to monetise your expertise, knowledge, and personality. My aim is to guide you through this book in taking intellectual leadership by developing a professional personal brand or even thought leadership.

Read, Listen, and Act

Podcast alert:

Listening to individuals who are actively engaged, with their feet firmly planted on the ground, is always insightful. Rather than just writing about them, I had conversations with them. That's why, in this book, you will encounter references to my podcast whenever there's a compelling discussion that enriches the topic or offers an alternative angle.

Take action:

This book is about awareness, discovery and reflection. If you want action steps, then take a look at my programmes on iankafleerackers.com and subscribe to the newsletter.

PART 1: DARE TO GET ATTENTION

I was attending a seminar by an American business coach at the Four Seasons Hotel in Fort Lauderdale, Florida when I decided to call a spade a spade and write that personal branding revolves around attention. Getting attention, giving attention, earning attention, provoking attention, avoiding attention, directing attention. And it is precisely this that poses the greatest stumbling block for many people: not knowing how to handle attention.

That's why I want to first delve into the various facets of attention. I invite you to pause and consider your personal stance and beliefs on this matter. It will clarify how you intend to deal with personal branding or what you need to change to build a strong personal brand.

Chapter 1: Everything is perception

Let me get straight to the point and make it very personal. When you look at yourself, do you recognise yourself best when you look in the mirror or at a photo of yourself? The answer is: your reflection in the mirror.

The mere-exposure effect

Because we see our reflection more often, pay attention to it, and become accustomed to it, we naturally start to appreciate it more; this is a phenomenon known in psychology as the mere-exposure effect. But there's more to it: the mirror shows us a reversed version of ourselves. We see right and left as opposites. The facial half that is on the right in the image is used for self-recognition, as research from University College Dublin shows. This is because the function of self-recognition resides in our left brain hemisphere.

When we look at a photo of ourselves, we unconsciously still focus on the right side but then see the other side of our face. And that is not the image we recognise from the mirror. We often can't quite put our finger on it, but it feels odd, different. We forget that we have various facial expressions. So when we see a photo of ourselves, we think: huh, that looks strange.

We have a perception of ourselves, an illusion that our appearance is constant. But the way we look depends on our mood and context. So, in reality, we don't even know what we truly look like. Colleagues, friends, and family do see all these different faces. They know what we look like when we're gloomy, jealous, or insecure. But also how we glow when we're overjoyed or in love. So they actually have a better idea of what we look like than we do ourselves. Yet, people don't look at us objectively either. Everyone views us through a lens, influenced by their experiences, cultural background, life history, personality traits, emotions, and their own illusion of themselves. They too form a perception of who we are.

The Looking Glass Self effect

But what if what we perceive matches reality? What if your behaviour and self-esteem are dictated by your predictions about how others see you? When it comes to understanding ourselves, social interaction plays a more crucial role than many of us realise. Sociologist Charles Horton Cooley suggests that individuals develop their self-image and sense of self-worth by observing how they are perceived by others, a concept he named the 'Looking Glass Self' (1902). People use the judgements of others in social interaction as a sort of mirror to measure their own value, values, and behaviour. This naturally implies that the 'self-concept' is not developed in isolation but within a social environment, indicating that society and the individual are inseparable.

The process of the 'Looking Glass Self' unfolds in three steps:
1. An individual in a social situation imagines how they appear to others.
2. That individual imagines other people's judgement of that appearance.
3. The individual develops feelings about that and reacts to these perceived judgements.

However, the process becomes more complex due to the multitude of contacts, the context of each interaction, and the nature of the individuals involved. Not all feedback, for example, carries the same weight. People may take the reactions of those they trust more seriously than those of strangers. Signals can be misinterpreted. People also usually consider their own value systems when thinking about changes in their behaviour or self-image.

Ultimately, the process of the Looking Glass Self is one of alignment, where you continuously strive to create congruence between your internal and external world. Thus, you spend your entire life observing, adjusting, and seeking balance.

The Cyber Self

Social media adds an infinitely more complex layer because it allows you to connect with others in ways you could never have imagined before. You now have not just one mirror but an ever-increasing number of mirrors.

> In 2017, Mary Aiken was one of the very first forensic cyberpsychologists to delve into people's online personalities. She introduced the concept of a 'cyberself', the version of oneself that someone chooses to present on a digital platform. Just like in real life, the cyberself can communicate with other individuals, receive social feedback, and conform to social norms. However, Aiken notes significant differences between the cyberself and the real self.

For instance, a person can have multiple versions of their cyberself. He or she might present a professional persona on LinkedIn, a casual one on Instagram, or an artistic one on Pinterest. And who knows how we will shape ourselves in the Metaverse. The cyberself also persists in social spaces, even when people are not interacting with those environments in real time. In this way, social media users are never fully shielded from exposure to judgement and critique. And unlike the real self, the cyberself is much more malleable when it comes to being shaped, updated, and perfected, for better or worse.

Of course 'you get only one chance to make a first impression'.

Social perception or interpersonal perception, there's no escaping it. We all live in a kind of matrix that we occasionally puncture. And then they hit you with this: "You only get one chance to make a first impression." What terrifying and ridiculous wordplay. Of course, you can only make a first impression once. You can also only make a second impression once. What did you expect? Do they mean you can only impress once?

A Princeton study from 2006 showed that the accuracy of a first impression someone makes on you is significant and unchangeable. In 2021, researchers came up with a more nuanced result. They studied the impact of first impressions on business relationships/partnerships and reached various conclusions. It will surprise no one that their research confirms first impressions are very important when it comes to building a trust relationship. However, the study also notes that a bad first impression does not always spell disaster. That first impression is mainly about detecting trust. Can this person be trusted or not? And with a feeling like trust, you're dealing with the reptilian brain that immediately wants to know if you're in danger and should attack, run away, or freeze. Are you safe with this person or not?

Now, I believe that this, too, should be taken with a pinch of salt. Because there's also the context in which a first impression occurs, as well as the personality and mood of the person making a judgement. Trust means different things to different people. Suppose you didn't do so well that first time. After all, you're only human. What's the secret to rectifying a bad first impression? A lot will depend on the actions that follow that first meeting to increase your 'trust' factor. And that takes time.

Can we change perception?

Based solely on a first impression, someone can form a judgement about you. A judgement that may extend far beyond those initial seconds, that one evening of conversation. For someone who doesn't possess a social superpower, this is a nightmare. Fortunately, with a few adjustments, you can mitigate the damage. Here are some of my tips:

1/ Ask friends and colleagues, people you trust and who will give you an honest answer, how they perceive you when you enter a room and meet new people. According to them, how do you behave? Compare this with what you experience yourself and think about what you want to change.

During my training sessions, I sometimes have my clients call their friends to ask them these questions. They always find it an embarrassing task because it's out of their comfort zone, but once they've done it, they receive valuable feedback. Moreover, they can hide behind the fact that their coach assigned the task. Self-awareness is always the first step in personality branding.

2/ Prepare yourself when you go to an event or meeting. Find out more about the guests attending. Think about relevant topics you could talk about.

As a moderator of events, researching people is always part of my job. I've also started doing it when I'm attending as a guest. It's a smart and handy trait if you quickly learn to connect with someone else's life. And remember: the connection can also be found in opposing interests. Then, it's important not to turn it into a game of right or wrong, but to enjoy the differences and the discussion.

3/ Enter the room calmly, look around before you proceed further into the room. It allows you to acclimatise. But at the same time, it gives others the chance to see you. I always think of animals that first smell each other from a distance and then come closer in a circular motion. But also of how the names of royals are announced when they stand in the doorway before entering. Two very different worlds, but both are intended to make encounters go smoothly.

4/ And then the most important part: smile. Practise an open, smiling expression at home. Think about what your face feels like when you're surprised, curious, or amazed. Look in the mirror and see what happens to your eyes and mouth. Your posture. A facial expression is a combination of muscle tension and emotion. Learn to feel this and reproduce the feeling. Work with muscle memory. Tone it down a bit, and you get an open look. The most beautiful and sincere smile is a Duchenne smile – a smile that reaches your eyes. The funny thing is that when you start practising such a smile, you also become happier. It's a contagious smile, one that inspires trust, and you know exactly what I mean if I refer to Julia Roberts. Her smile is worth gold. But so is yours.

This is a more conscious approach to giving a 'first impression' and correcting a less favourable impression through subsequent actions. These are four points you can address to influence the perception others form of you, but there's more. It's about getting a foot in the door, which is crucial. Creating your own opportunities so that people can get to know you better, rather than depending on the opportunities others offer to make yourself known. Taking the initiative yourself and ensuring that people have the chance to get to know you better, even if you're not physically present. That's where the strength of personal branding lies.

Reputation

A first impression is made in contact with others. But what if you're not there? In a book about personal branding, you're bound to come across the following quote by Jeff Bezos: "Your brand is what people say about you when you're not in the room." And it seems that if Bezos says it, then it must be true. It definitely fits into the narrative of anyone involved with personal branding, just as the first impression quote fits that of body language experts, and the fear of public speaking quote suits public speaking coaches. These are quotes that I like to examine closely.

When you ask yourself what people might talk about when they discuss (or gossip about) you, it leads to the experiences they've had with you and the perception they've acquired from those experiences. People will make their own thing out of it, and since you're not in the room, they'll do with it what they want. And that turns out to be the definition of reputation.

> ***"Reputation is the overall quality or character as seen or judged by people in general."***
> (Merriam-Webster)

> ***"The opinion that people have of someone or something, based on past behaviour or character."***
> (Cambridge dictionary)

Although reputation and personal brand overlap, they are two different things. Most people first have a reputation and may opt for a personal brand. Most personal brands do have a reputation. Generations born with a smartphone in their cradle do it differently. Because they start working on their cyberself at a young age, they tend to think they have a personal brand sooner. This does not always have advantages, but they will find that out later on in life.

If your reputation as a business leader comes under fire, then a communication expert will work on reputation management, which means adjusting what was said. Putting out fires, calming tempers, issuing corrections, arranging interviews... And if your reputation as an employee or job seeker comes under fire, you face gossip, evaluations, dismissal, fewer job offers... Scary, isn't it?

All of that can be less necessary when you are building the narrative yourself. When you are omnipresent, whether you're in the room or not, people can get to know you at any time. That is what personal branding is all about. But don't get it wrong: personal branding is a verb, a process. It doesn't necessarily make you a personal brand. That, in turn, is a status.

But what about Bezos? Well, he probably gave that quote at a time when he (or Amazon) was already a brand and there was no need to distinguish between brand and reputation. When your personal brand becomes much stronger and more visible to people who haven't even met you, that naturally becomes what people talk about. But since you are reading this book, you're not yet at that stage.

Now that we're on the subject of language, there are other words that cause confusion and overlap: personal branding, reputation, PR, reputation management, image, perception, influencer marketing. But when do you use what? Depending on who you're talking to, different jargon will be put forward, simply because that word is used as a keyword within the framework in which this professional operates.

To give an example:

> You'll mostly encounter 'personal branding' when speaking with someone who will take care of your online marketing and online visibility. If you're talking to someone mainly concerned with crisis communication and credibility, then they'll talk about reputation. Nowadays, it's trendy to call yourself a personal branding photographer and stylist. If you're talking to a professional working on emotional intelligence, you're likely to hear the word perception more quickly. Do they all talk about the same thing? Yes. No. "There's overlap, but the focus is different," you'll hear them say in podcasts.

The word you use can also depend on the social circles you wish to move into. There are quite a few executives who think that focusing on 'personal branding' is too commercial and contrived, while concentrating

Reputation is the overall quality or character as seen or judged by people in general

(Merriam-Webster)

on your 'reputation' is much more serious. To ensure that you understand exactly what I mean by each word while reading this book, I will share my vision/meaning of the words. This is based on my experience in media and business, rather than on what others say.

Here we go:

Perception: Everything starts with perception. In your interactions with people, you form impressions of them, and they of you. This impression creates a perception. It's a snapshot of an experience you've had with this person or that someone had with you.

Reputation: You build a reputation when others can see a clear connection between your actions, your behaviour and the perceptions they have of you. However, it can vary depending on the observer's perceptions or the circles they belong to.

Reputation management: The actions taken to control and adjust the conversation about you. For this, you either work on the situations where things went wrong: for example, monitoring and addressing online complaints, sending a press release with corrections, apologies... or you go back to the drawing board and revise the vision around your personal brand.

Public relations: Your efforts to be heard by someone else's audience. By this, I mean: guest appearances on podcasts, interviews in magazines, panel discussions on television, keynotes at events...

Influencer marketing: An influencer is someone who can affect the purchasing power of others. Influencer marketing is a form of social media marketing where companies and brands engage individuals to promote their products. These individuals have an influence on the actions of their social media audience. A personal brand will not necessarily promote other brands, but an influencer will.

Personal Branding is the collection of all the actions YOU undertake to steer the perception people have of you through what you communicate, how you communicate, when you communicate, how you visualise yourself, how you make yourself heard, and how you make yourself recognisable (in style of typography, website, clothing, certain words, behaviour, photography...).

In other words:

- People always have perceptions of themselves and others.
- You can have a reputation without being a personal brand.
- You can start the personal branding process without having a reputation.
- Personal branding equals being visible and handling attention.

If you want to thrive in a business context, it's crucial that people know you, trust you, and appreciate you. Take the initiative yourself, because you don't want to leave determining and passing this on entirely to others. Building a strong reputation is essential if you want to be successful. And to become visible and support your reputation, you shape it through your personal branding.

The question I will ask you in the next chapter is: do you dare to be visible?

Summary of Chapter 1: Everything is perception

7 things to remember:

1. Accept that everything is perception – both for you and for others.
2. The perception people have of you determines your reputation.
3. People always have perceptions of themselves and others.
4. You can have a reputation without being a personal brand.
5. You can start the personal branding process without having a reputation.
6. Personal branding is the collection of actions you take to drive that perception.
7. Personal branding equals being visible and handling attention.

Chapter 2: Dare to be visible

In addition to my work as an actor, I had to deal with the 'peripheral activities', like red carpet events, press conferences, media reviews, and encounters with fans. These activities had a profound impact on me both as a professional and as a young woman. I had to figure out how to handle attention that seemed excessive, sometimes well-intentioned, other times not to be trusted. It was a tightrope walk in finding a balance in being myself, protecting but also showing myself, while simultaneously meeting the expectations others had of me, and considering how to build financial security from it that made me happy. I was very deliberate about the professional choices I made, who I wanted to collaborate with, what I told journalists, how I behaved at parties, how I looked, and was meticulous in reviewing press articles. No one taught me this, but I had strong intuition, was sober-minded, and could spot red flags from a distance. My reputation was my greatest asset. At that time, I did not realise I was working on my personal brand. That came to my attention years later when Boston Consulting Group asked me to give a keynote on personal branding.

In the second phase of my professional life, I guided entrepreneurs, leaders, and experts who had stepped into the spotlight by delivering keynotes and giving interviews. I taught them to recognise the pitfalls, create mental safety, and have an impact with their story. But I noticed that most of them did not consider the concept of personal branding; they looked no further than the keynote they would give. On the other hand, their expectations for this single performance were sky-high.

They also failed to see the connection between shining on stage, what they shared online, and the revenue model they worked with on a daily basis. Often, these aspects were at odds with one another. And that's not even mentioning their personal quality of life, which was at stake as a result of all the balls they were juggling.

In my group training sessions, I often encounter people who want to overcome their fear of public speaking. They usually think that they need to change their posture, work on their voice, and figure out what to do with their hands. According to one study, people are said to fear public speaking more than death. The study dates back to 1973 and was conducted in a questionable manner. But it sounded so convincing that, to this day, that result is still liberally used to promote social anxiety therapy and public speaking training.

The American comedian Jerry Seinfeld addressed this in one of his stand-ups:

> "Speaking in public is often cited as the number one fear of adults. The Book of Lists places the fear of death in fifth place while public speaking ranks first. That would mean at a funeral, people are five times more likely to want to be in the casket than giving the eulogy."

I don't believe in the fear of public speaking. Public speaking is not a mandatory life skill. No one, not even your boss, can force you into it, though it is an important career-building skill. The fear of going outside is much more crucial to address, but not the fear of going on stage.

So, if you decide to tackle it, then please define the fear correctly. Is it fear or uncertainty due to a lack of skills and practice? Most likely the latter. Don't make it bigger than it is; that's not healthy.

The Triangle of Fear in personal branding

There are underlying insecurities that you're not aware of and almost no one says out loud. I encounter them even with professionals who are considering starting their personal branding. There are three of them; I call them The Triangle of Fear in personal branding, and I invite you to pause and reflect on each of them and how they apply to you.

FOPO: Fear of other people's opinions

When you stand on a stage and look into the room, you see all those eyes looking at you. If you've ever seen the musical *Cats*, then you surely remember the scene of the Jellicle cats in the dark – a beautiful image of all those flickering, glowing cat eyes. Quite scary, too.

When you experience this for the first time, your reptilian brain kicks into action: you want to flee, fight, or freeze. Something in your primal brain thinks this could possibly be dangerous. Now, as a modern human, you can rationalise this, and you realise that this room full of people will not attack you – at least not physically. What they possibly *will* do, however, is have an opinion about what you're doing, how you do it, and what you say. And we call that feeling of fear FOPO, fear of other people's opinions.

- What are they going to say about me?
- They might tune out because...
- I don't want them to know what I do beforehand.
- I want to see their reactions.
- I don't want to be judged behind my back.

Getting a grip on this feeling is an action point for the professionals I train. And while you have more direct communication tools at your disposal in an offline world – your voice, your body, your language, your intonation, your energy – and you can also get more feedback from the body language of the receiver of your message, this is much less often the case in the online world.

FOPO prevents many professionals from sharing their opinions or a life or work experience. For CEOs, it is THE reason to remain invisible. They mainly look at what happens to others and how the general public reacts.

One of my favourite examples is Elon Musk. Musk is a typical example of a professional who is praised to the skies one day and vilified the next. The price of his stocks follows suit. But the man himself doesn't give a darn about the opinions of others, as I was told by someone from his network. And you can see that because he continues to follow his own course.

Receiving criticism is not equally easy for everyone. It is a learning process that also depends on your character and upbringing. When someone leaves a critical comment on a post/keynote/book, the following reactions can pop up:

- You freeze and don't dare anymore.
- You become temporarily obsessed with this person.

You experience feelings of anger, powerlessness, and inferiority. You can learn how to cope with this but you also have to realise you always have a choice. You can choose not to publish. That way you avoid comments, but you will remain invisible. You can choose not to read the comments, or not to respond to them and let the storm pass.

Tall trees catch a lot of wind. Really tall trees must withstand storms. Those 'opinions' will come regardless. The question is: do you leave what is said about you entirely up to others, or do you give people a chance to get to know you better so that what is said about you can also be measured against the things you say? But FOPO is not the fear you should tackle first. There is another one that is more important and can reduce FOPO.

FOOO: Fear of my own opinion

After giving a keynote on personal branding, one person pointed out these issues to me: "There are so many voices shouting on LinkedIn." "Consistent posting takes so much time." "There is so much noise." "Some people post so much that you wonder what their intention and essence really is." I understand what they are feeling, but in our criticism of others, we deny ourselves opportunities.

Do you realise to what extent this way of thinking prevents you from planting your flag and making your voice heard? What makes you think that you will do it in the same way? Are you afraid of your own opinion?

What if you translated your annoyance into questions that help you move forward instead of holding you back? How do I ensure my voice sounds different? How do I make sure that consistent posting is also efficient? How do I ensure that my essence comes across clearly?

It's easy to have an opinion, to criticise, and to do nothing about it yourself. If something in someone irritates you, then it's an interesting exercise to discover exactly what that is and why. Often, you'll find answers along the lines of: she does something I ought to be doing. He doesn't have as much experience as I do, yet he is more successful. He has more opportunities than I do. She has staff for that; she doesn't do it herself.

A comment I constantly receive is this: yes, but it's different/easier for you because you're a media professional. What people don't realise is that I worked in television for 30 years to get that status. And while this 'status' is the result of work and performance, at the same time it's a curse because it creates obstacles, and also closes doors.

Such remarks allow one to avoid decision-making, because choosing means losing, committing to one thing and not another. So think about that, what reasons do you have to avoid making choices?

FOSO: Fear of standing out

Fear of other people's opinions is the easiest to identify. Fear of your own opinion is more of an ego thing and somewhat harder to admit. But the fear that blocks the path to your success as a personality brand (and keynote speaker) is FOSO, the fear of standing out. Do you dare to be visible? Many people keep themselves small, settle for less, suppress desires, dreams, talents. Why? They are afraid to stand out. They have this perception of what can go wrong and become insecure because of it. Mostly they are not self-aware enough.

What if you become successful but can't handle it? What if you expect to become successful but then it turns out not to be the case?

> You might not realise it, but becoming successful can also be very intimidating for you (and your loved ones). Think about all those stars (singers, actors, YouTubers...) who lose their way when fame becomes too much for them. From my own life, I can tell you that in the '90s, I evolved from a redhead who was laughed at and bullied to the most famous redhead in the country, whom boys and men fell in love with, and mothers named their newborns after. Someone who could no longer walk the streets without being recognised and to whom the most bizarre questions were asked. To give you an example: "Would you donate your underwear to our charity event?"

In *The Big Leap*, Gay Hendricks describes how we all too often prefer to play it safe in our 'zone of excellence', the zone where we do what we are good at and where we are appreciated, but also where we are kept small by ourselves and others. And this while we would be much more successful (and happier) in our Zone Of Genius.

Can you handle success? Can you handle being a strong, controversial personal brand?

Should you know the answer to this question in advance? There is a world of difference between knowing and experiencing. It is important to stay true to yourself and loyal to your values, virtues, and how you want to live your life.

FOSO is often culturally bound and driven by the environment in which you live and work. Change that environment to one that motivates and supports you and find a mentor who knows what it's like to lead such a life.

You must work on your Triangle of Fear to engage in personal branding. The best and easiest way to achieve this is by addressing the fear of your own opinion. Get rid of that fear, and you will feel far less uncertain with the other two.

You simply CANNOT be invisible. What is possible, however, is to decide how you want to be visible. How you shape your personal brand is up to you.

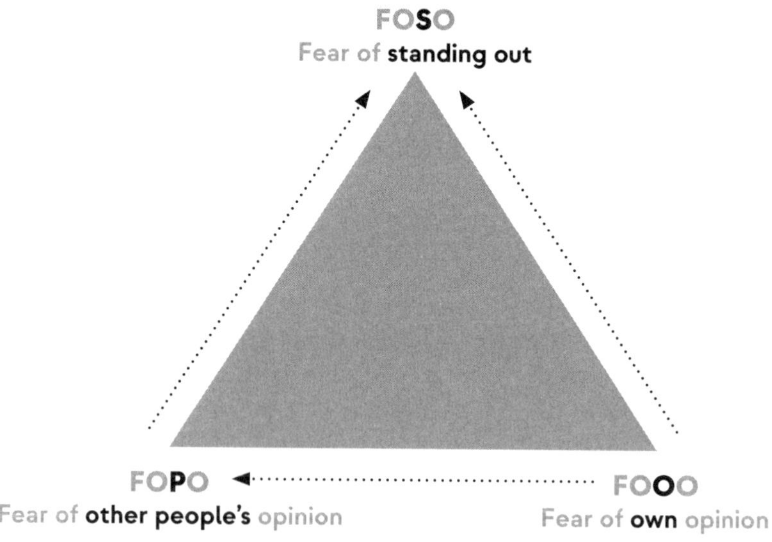

The Triangle of Fear.
Working on your FOOO helps solve the other two.

The dark side

Attention is a pendulum that can go from everything to nothing. Absolutely nothing... You might not realise this, but people who choose not to be visible on the internet, people who decide not to have social media accounts, do exist. But it can go even further. You can also decide to be erased from the archives of the internet. As a citizen, you do indeed have the right to be forgotten. "The right to be forgotten."

To give you an example: in Belgium, Google approved the request to remove a 19-year-old news article about a victim of an assault to protect the identity of the young victim. In a ruling from May 2014, the Court of Justice of the European Union decided that individuals have the right to ask search engines like Google to remove certain results about them. Between 2014 and 2023, this has amounted to 5,435,112 URLs, and the number of requests continues to rise. That's one extreme. The other extreme is that of unexpected success that seems to happen overnight.

Trading attention

Those who decide to be visible not only find it okay to attract attention but also actively seek it. And preferably the right kind. *Everyone Famous*, the title of the Oscar-nominated Belgian film from 2000 by Belgian filmmaker Dominique de Ruddere, in which I had the pleasure of playing a small role, is now a reality. Social media gives everyone their five minutes of fame. Today, everyone active on social media is unconsciously seeking attention. Many children dream of becoming a princess. The chance of actually becoming one is almost none; the chance of portraying one in a series that would be rebroadcast for 30 years was mine. But thanks to social media, every girl or boy can at least act like one and even gain likes, followers (and revenue).

Dag

When you live a life of visibility, you have to learn to deal with it. It takes over your life and turns it upside down. Unfortunately, I see most people blindly falling into the trap and completely indulging in attention until they hit rock bottom. Only then do they pass on the lessons learned with an air of great wisdom. Personal branding can lead you in this direction. You have to be vigilant that the personal brand you create can be sustained and nurtured. I find "fake it till you make it" the worst advice you can get. Unthoughtful. And those who give this advice often also hold authenticity in high esteem. I see too many people getting stuck by it. No wonder...

Before the internet, talking about personal brands typically referred only to celebrities and stars who made it onto television, the stage, or into newspapers. And that was only possible if you were singled out from the crowd because of your achievements, notable statements and appearance, or scandals. Your reputation was then equal to your personal brand. There was nothing between your achievements and what was said about you. And actually, the term personal branding itself only came into use in 1997, when Tom Peters coined it. He saw it as a necessity for employees to make themselves visible in the job market. But his vision and effort didn't have much success.

In 2023, it's different again. Now, personal branding seems to be only about how you behave on social media. Everyone can now easily run a media company, with their own newspaper, TV, and virtual stage by simply being present on a social media platform. Between your real-life achievements and what is said about you now also lies what you post and show on other platforms. In other words, you have multiple 'touchpoints' at your disposal to shape your personal brand and thus steer your reputation. And that's a good thing. It's necessary.

We live in an attention economy, an economic system where human attention is traded, captured, and monetised. The concept of an *'attention economy'* existed even before the internet. Herbert Simon, an economist and cognitive psychologist, argued in the 1970s that in a world full of information, the most valuable commodity is human attention, and the ability to capture people's attention is a crucial factor for success across various fields.

Before the internet, the attention economy was primarily driven by traditional media such as television, radio, and print. Companies and brands competed for a share of people's attention by advertising on these platforms, creating content to be broadcasted or printed, and building their reputation through public relations.

You gain a different insight into your experiences when you let time pass and adopt a helicopter view. You could say that information was scarcer back then. In other words, if you wanted attention, you had to stand on a box in the park and proclaim your message. People would listen because you had new information. If you did that now, no one would listen because information is much more easily and abundantly available, and attention has become much scarcer.

If Simon thought there was a lot of information available back then, what would he think now that there is a tsunami of information and content on the internet and social media? Moreover, it's not just companies and brands competing for consumer attention, but also individuals themselves who, with their tricks, knowledge, experiences, and stories, want a piece of the attention pie. Tom Peters can finally rub his hands together because what he foresaw in 1997 has finally become a problem.

If you want to attract attention, you need to create content.

On the one hand, there is too much information, but on the other hand, the internet has made it easier for individuals and companies to create and distribute content. The influencer economy grew at a rapid pace, leaving professionals in the business world watching from the sidelines. What they did, the influence they had, and the often massive revenues involved made professionals, entrepreneurs, and even companies envious. Influencers were scoffed at, even as they were simultaneously enlisted to promote brands. What did they do that wasn't happening in the business world yet? They knew how to put themselves in the spotlight using technology. They were also content creators, which allowed them to build a loyal community around their persona. Through this persona-bound community, they were able to earn a lot of money.

These influencers are part of the creator economy and have paved the way for a new approach to personal branding online. While influencers are known for promoting other people's products within their own community and leveraging their personality for this purpose, the creator economy also includes content creators who aim to promote their intellectual, artistic, or practical knowledge and expertise.

The creator economy refers to economic activities based on creativity, knowledge, and intellectual property. It thrives on innovation, originality, and cultural expression. Thanks to the development of various software and technology that made production accessible to everyone, new business models emerged, and global sales became possible. Although personal branding predates the internet, the most significant breakthrough came with the rise of the creator economy.

Personal branding is the process of creating and promoting a clear image and reputation for yourself in the professional market. By developing your own narrative, not just offline but especially online, you can distinguish yourself as an individual and position yourself as an expert in your field, which can lead to greater visibility, opportunities, and ultimately, success. Many professionals, especially those with a track record of more than ten years, still fail to realise that personal branding requires content. A lot of content.

Summary of Chapter 2: Dare to be different

A few things to remember: Learn to deal with the Triple F, three fears that prevent many people from stepping into a personal branding process.

1. Fear of other people's opinions
2. Fear of standing out
3. Fear of your own opinion

If you want to start your personal branding process, you are entering the attention economy. This means:

1. You have to dare to be different.
2. You have to dare to be visible.
3. You need to create content.

PART 2: WHY

In a world bombarded with Simon Sinek's advice, *Start with Why* (2009), the why question in personal branding is the very first question that pops into most professionals' minds.

Why should I bother?

Personal branding has a bad reputation and makes people think of egotism, self-glorification. Personal branding needs rebranding itself. The reason for this, in my opinion, is that people are too seldom able to give it their own personal interpretation and mostly look at the examples available. Due to their insecurity, they are more likely to cling to the examples that scare them the most. In their audacity, they identify with an idol who has 'made it completely' or someone who caused a scandal.

My goal in this book is to provide you with a vision built on a life in the public eye, through working in many different industries that are still in their infancy in terms of experience with visibility, combined with the study of people dealing with social media. I hope that by reading this book, you will discover what it can and should mean for you. In the following chapter, I want to help you find an answer to your why question. This answer will vary depending on the professional role you play. By this I mean: whether you are an employee, a solo entrepreneur, or an executive/CEO.

Why should I bother?

Chapter 3: Personal branding as a growth marketing strategy

Why should you, as a solopreneur, engage in personal branding?

As a solo entrepreneur, you are your most important asset. This often makes it confusing. You are BOTH your business, AND your product, AND your CEO. You negotiate about yourself with prospects, you advertise yourself on social media.

For service-providing solo entrepreneurs, being 'taken seriously' is an important point. That is one of the reasons why they present themselves using a company name. Using a company name sounds much more professional to them than saying that John Johnson provides the services.

But it's rare for your network and your customers to use that company name. They will much sooner mention your name. It is also more difficult to make a company known than a person because social media is aimed at networking and making contact between people. As soon as you want to start as a company, you get more restrictions from algorithms, unless you start using paid ads.

It becomes completely crazy when you realise that companies are doing the exact opposite in their branding and are increasingly giving it a human touch and perspective. Why? Because people buy from people.

Because people trust what other people say about a product. And because a person is seen.

Another reason why solopreneurs choose to offer their services under a company name is because of their ambition to sell their business later in life. Some say that a company that bears the personal name of or revolves around one person is more difficult or even impossible to sell. But what about makeup artist Bobbi Brown or fashion designer Dries Van Noten, who sold their company, brand (and name)?

PODCAST ALERT
In my podcast, I talk to professionals, like entrepreneur **Andy Coomans**, who help companies prepare for an exit strategy.

I also faced this dilemma myself; my personal brand immediately took precedence over my 'Thought Leaders Academy'. Time and again, I was told that I should build my business using my personal brand, while I preferred not to. It turned out to be the fastest way and it's not irreversible. You can develop a thriving business from your personal brand and then give it a different name once you can let it continue as a self-sustaining entity. It then gives you the space to explore new horizons with your personal brand.

Every solopreneur would do well to step into the process of personal branding. After all, a certain level of recognition and a network are necessary to keep working. Often, I meet proud new consultants who have left their well-paying corporate jobs for the more adventurous free life of a consultant. They then tell me that they don't need to promote themselves online. After all, their agenda is already full with one or two recurring clients. They don't realise that they have left one golden cage for a gilded one, one where the gold disappears once the client leaves. They take word-of-mouth advertising for granted and love being the best-kept secret of two clients.

Another reason why personal branding is important is because, as a solo entrepreneur, you sell services that do not differ much from other service providers in terms of content. Think of LinkedIn trainers, life coaches, business coaches. There may be a difference in methods, in the depth of knowledge transfer, in the format of the knowledge transfer, in price, but the decisive differentiator that will make others choose you is your personality, style, vision, and approach. And you show and let these flourish in your personal branding journey.

> For example
> I am known as a professional with both broad and deep expertise, someone who approaches work pragmatically and teaches you to think metacognitively. I challenge, am direct, and do not shy away from discussions. No fluff. I don't see myself as a coach, but as a mentor, fresh-eye provider, sparring partner, contrarian. When I talk to a prospect, I soon know whether we are a match. I'm using my personal branding process to filter my prospects and to ensure that the chance of a match is already high when someone schedules a call in my agenda. This way, we both waste the least time and energy. YOLO.

As a solo entrepreneur, your time is your most valuable asset. Through your personal branding, you can ensure that you take control of your time, that your reach can grow, and that you can plant the seeds for the moment you want to scale up. Because believe me, that day will come.

Why CEOs and C-suite executives need to engage in personal branding

But what about the leaders of a company: the CEO and their C-suite? The professionals who are overseeing teams and are accountable to a board of directors. Professionals whose decisions and actions can impact revenue, investments, and even IPOs. But also: professionals who often don't engage in the social media scene because they have a communications and marketing department. Who, in their role, also face responsibilities that can be legally contested.

In my meetings and work with executives and CEOs, I hear stories like these:

> One CEO confided in me that boards of directors often are not keen on CEOs who attract attention. They shouldn't have too strong an opinion, it was said.
>
> And another told me that when he posted on LinkedIn, his team told him he should be working instead of doing that.
>
> From a communications worker in an international corporate, I hear that they wish their CEO would embody and express more thought leadership.
>
> When I, as a moderator of corporate events, call CEOs to the stage for a discussion or a speech, I regretfully must note all too often how few are charismatic, approachable, and inspiring.

What is going wrong, I wonder. Isn't it the purpose that, as captain of the ship, you are a role model for your people? Isn't that what leading is about? Or is a Chief Executive Officer just as the title indicates: executive, engaged in strategy and operational matters? What's not mentioned in their job description is that they should actually also be Chief Brand Ambassadors and, in the best case, Chief Visionary Officers. Or at least, that's what I would expect from them if I were to invest money and time in them. And it turns out I'm not the only one.

The main reason to go for it

Ask entrepreneurs about the essence of business, and they will say 'trust'. Without trust, there's no business. What are the two most important currencies that stakeholders in your company won't part with when trust is lacking? Time and money. The stakeholders in a company are your investors, your customers, and your employees. The first two 'give' you their money when they trust you. The latter gives you their time. You really need to be worth it.

Let's look at what is needed to gain the trust of investors and customers so that they invest in your company or products.

Investors

In the first years after I had ended my career as an actress, I worked on a wild concept that would connect technology and literature. These two industries are to each other like robots are to dinosaurs.

As a passionate reader and author, I wanted to promote reading among children by developing a digital platform where children's literature was offered through gamification. I saw how children were not stimulated by all those white pages full of lines with letters. It was just boring. The difference between the games they played at home, where they fought from one level to the next to gather more powers and learn skills, was much more exciting.

I had the opportunity to develop my idea at iMinds (now Imec) under the guidance of mentors. One of these mentors was a British venture capitalist. He was thrilled about how I pitched my idea with so much passion. I kept silent about my background and chuckled.

During one of our conversations, he told me that initially he looks at who is behind the idea, who is the captain of the ship, and whether they have the drive and strength to execute this idea. Passion was not something I lacked, but finding a suitable team in an industry I was completely unfamiliar with was a different challenge. I struggled with this, and when I pitched my idea to international keynote speaker, investor and serial entrepreneur Peter Hinssen, whom I had trained at the time, he too immediately pointed out the critical issue. In the end, nothing came of the original idea, but I did manage to launch two derivative products in the market, including the first interactive picture book on iPad at the launch of the tablet in Belgium. Preschoolers could determine the course of the story themselves through the choices they made. The app remained at number 1 in the iTunes Store for months and sold worldwide.

A second derivative was the publishing house iStoires, which I started with Rosemie Callewaert, coordinator of innovation and development at the University Library Ghent. iStoires published digital-first short stories from well-known authors that served as a marketing tool for their work. Schools eagerly utilised the new material. We also came out with an original print version. Together with the City of Ostend, we developed a city marketing concept using short stories that saw two editions.

Back to the investors. Later, when I began conducting pitch training at incubators and accelerators and engaged in conversations with investors again, I heard the same sentiment, but this time with a notable statement: first the person, then the business. You can always work on the business plan and the product, as long as there is enough potential and a market for it. But if the founders don't stand strong, it invariably ends badly. They told me that's why it was important for them to learn more about the founders.

I recently heard the same story again when I was training the investment managers of a publicly traded investment fund. In their research phase, they also investigated who the founders were. And they conducted part of that research online.

There are certain milestones in a person's life. While our era counts from Before Christ and After Christ, in a person's life, you have before you had children, and after you had children, and, depending on where you live, for example, before 9/11 and after 9/11.

But globally, we also have before COVID and after COVID. And in a few years, we could say the same about the breakthrough of generative AI, but that's a whole different discussion. With the COVID milestone, we have a special one: there is not only a before and an after but also a during. In reviewing research, professional literature, and online publications, I have chosen not to use data or studies published before the pandemic in 2020 unless they could be used for comparison with the present. The world has changed too much in terms of leadership.

In their 2023 digital Investor Survey, Brunswick, a leading public relations and communications company, investigated how institutional investors search for information online, how they evaluate a company's digital presence, and the impact of that information on their investment decisions. They took a global sample of 257 institutional investors from the US, the UK, Canada, and the EU from large and small investment firms.

I highlight the key insights regarding online presence:

1. **Corporate websites:** They form the foundation of effective digital communication. 84% of investors consider company websites as the primary source of information for investment research. Therefore, maintaining an up-to-date, user-friendly, and responsive website is of fundamental importance.

2. **The growing influence of social media:** 67% of investors now use social media for investment research. Companies must therefore have a strong presence on popular platforms like LinkedIn, X (formerly Twitter), and YouTube to effectively engage with investors and enhance their online visibility.

3. **Preferred social media platforms for investors:** LinkedIn (81%), X, formerly Twitter (71%), and YouTube (68%) emerge as the top three social media platforms for investors. Companies should utilise these platforms to share updates and engage in conversations.

4. **The importance of digital events and webinars:** 70% of respondents attended digital events in the past year, and 65% believe these will remain relevant post-pandemic. This means companies need to include digital events and webinars in their IR strategy to

maintain regular contact with investors and provide good access to management.

5. **The rise of podcasts and livestreams:** 43% of investors tune into podcasts and 37% participate in livestreams for investment information. Companies should explore these formats to provide investors with easy and accessible information.

These insights highlight the importance of a company's online presence for investors. The research also looked at what investors expect from CEOs. The impact and significance of a CEO's online visibility have dramatically increased since their previous research in 2019. Investors want to hear the news directly from the CEO and executives to gain trust. In practice, building an effective individual digital profile has not only become an essential part of a successful investor relations strategy, but it is now also a necessity to maintain shareholder value and compete with peers who are more active in digital and social media, according to Brunswick. I did my best to avoid confirmation bias and looked for studies that proved the contrary, but I didn't find any. Not just one but multiple studies indicated that a CEO's online presence influenced investors' decisions. And actually, that's not so strange. If you want to be able to trust someone, you want to get to know that person. You will not follow someone you don't trust. If you, as a CEO, do not offer sufficient opportunities to be known, then you are shooting yourself in the foot. And avoiding an online presence is a seriously missed opportunity.

Brunswick Insight published The Connected Leaders Survey in 2022, interviewing 2,800 readers of financial publications and 3,600 employees from companies with over 1,000 employees about their expectations regarding their leaders' communication. This was conducted in seven different countries and markets: Germany, Hong Kong SAR, Saudi Arabia, Singapore, the United Arab Emirates, the United Kingdom, and the United States. Propel, a reputable Australian reputation management advisory firm, also published a report examining and surveying the online presence of ASX 200 CEOs and executives on LinkedIn. The ASX 200 is a stock market index that contains the top 200 largest companies in Australia. The conclusion was the same each time: stakeholders expect executives to use social media to lead. Therefore, gaining investors' trust is one of the reasons why you as a leader (CEO or executive) might work on an online presence and personal brand.

But what if you don't need investors? Then you still have another stakeholder in your company whose money you need and whose trust you must gain: your customer.

Your customers

Decades ago, consumers simply chose the product that appealed to them the most. Selection could be based on quality or price. Over the years, as products became similar in quality, product marketing played the decisive role. Then we faced climate change, with ESG (Environmental, Social, and Corporate Governance) considerations, and companies were scrutinised on how they addressed these issues. And now, we are increasingly sceptical of what a company tells us. Company branding may sound great, but does it hold up behind the scenes? More and more often, consumers are watching the face of the company. How credible and genuine is this person, am I willing to follow them and trust them with my money?

Your (Future) Employees

And then there's the stakeholder who gives their time to your company. Due to COVID and the entry of Gen Z into the workforce, the working population now has a different approach to work. Am I willing to give my time to this company if I don't even like the leader?

A few years ago, I faced a dilemma. I was invited for an exploratory conversation at an international company. There was an attractive assignment waiting for me where I could train executives in public speaking across three countries. My thinking-out-of-the-box approach and experience in the media and artistic world interested them. However, during the conversation, I encountered one red flag after another. I discussed it with my brother-in-law, who was a CEO, and he advised me to look at the CEO, because he determines the company culture. I did as he suggested and found… nothing. The man was invisible except for a few press releases. I declined the assignment.

I am certainly not alone in thinking this way. According to the Edelman Trust Barometer of 2022, 92% of employees expect their CEO to speak out on topics such as the impact of automation on jobs, diversity, climate change, income inequality, the ethical use of technology, and on-the-job training. 81% believe that he/she should be personally visible and brave enough to discuss these topics publicly. In other words: increasingly, customers but especially employees want more assurance that the leader they follow is worth giving their time to. You only live once, as you know…

All well and good… but how do Belgian and Dutch CEOs respond to this? "Just act normal, that's already crazy enough," they say in the Netherlands. In Belgium, the saying goes, "Vivons heureux, vivons cachés" (live happily, live hidden). I didn't find extensive research on the topic, but at Finn, a Belgian communication agency specialising in strategic and corporate communication, I found a thesis at the Rotterdam School of Management, Erasmus University, from 2019 by communication professional Marisa Shaba. She interviewed 15 CEOs and board members of large Dutch companies about what she calls CEO activism. CEO activism is the practice where CEOs take public stances on environmental, social, and political issues that are not directly related to their business. She wanted to explore the extent to which the US trend around CEO activism would also spread to the Low Countries and possibly impact the corporate communication function. The conclusion of her small study was that Dutch CEOs were not keen on taking on and individually expressing views on societal themes.

The fear of taking the plunge is significant, especially when it concerns a large company and there's a risk of stepping on many toes. It could turn out very well but also poorly for the CEO and the company, so they prefer to be cautious by not engaging in it. This confirms what I hear and see in my work with leaders as a moderator and public speaking coach.

But as a CEO, you must be from another planet if you haven't realised that COVID has changed all this. Initially, we thought it was mainly the millennials who expected leaders to take a stance and be visible on social media. During the pandemic, it became clear they were not the only ones.

Meanwhile, Gen Z – a generation that is entirely critical when it comes to giving their time to people and companies they disagree with – is entering the workforce. What if you are the CEO of a privately held company? You lead a large or smaller company, or you are the founder-entrepreneur and boss of your business.

Captains of industry and entrepreneurs are less afraid of personal branding and can speak more freely, according to Shaba. But do they actually do it? Clearly not enough, otherwise I wouldn't be writing this book. The fear is so ingrained that only a few entrepreneurs hesitantly make their voices heard. Does it really have to be about societal themes? Of course not. The essence of the research I mention is that the investor, the customer, and the employee want to get to know you as a leader. And that the decisions made are partly determined by this. It's up to you to consider what kind of profile you want to adopt, which themes you want to address, and especially why. Ask yourself how people can and should get to know you better. What can you communicate, and what could be the added value of that on a professional, societal, but also human level? Don't forget, you don't have to be alone in this game; there are communication experts who can assist you.

More and more industries are engaging in the war for talent. Since COVID, people have become more aware of what they no longer want to do with their lives and work. It turns out to be not so easy to attract talent.

As part of the war for talent, iVox conducted a study commissioned by SD Worx on how European employers deal with attracting employees.

The research focuses on attractive employer branding in the war for talent, examining what employees look for in an employer and what employers focus on to become an attractive employer. The study found that 65% of Belgian employers struggle to attract employees. 7 out of 10 employers can't find suitable profiles.

Company leaders are facing a problem. And for that problem, there is already a solution: as a company, you need to ensure that talent feels drawn to join you. You need to become an attractive employer. In marketing, this is called employer branding. It encompasses creating a strong, positive image of the company, its culture, and its values. It helps to attract job seekers who align with the mission and objectives of the company.

To achieve this, companies rely on their employees, hoping to motivate them to become brand ambassadors. This process alone necessitates training and pathways to get people to that point.

But it turns out that it is not that easy to motivate employees in joining the employer branding programme. Here are a few good reasons:

- Employees only put something online if they believe in it and are satisfied with it;
- Employees only want to be brand ambassadors if their boss is the Chief Brand Ambassador;
- Moreover, it will only work when an employee has his own individual voice and online presence – read: follows a personal branding journey – that exists independently of their employer. Nobody wants to be used as a free advertising bunny.

So, even though employer branding is a marketing strategy, it doesn't start in the mind of a communication agency. It begins with the company culture, how people feel within the company, and if they can and are allowed to express themselves. It's about how visible and accessible the CEO is and sets an example.

PODCAST ALERT
Listen to the episodes where I talk about employer branding with my guests.

Where do the pitfalls and opportunities lie?

Zero or hero? What is the real risk?

While anonymity remains the most used survival strategy for the majority of CEOs, and boards might prefer a leader who avoids the spotlight, there are CEOs who are indeed visible. Which approach is then best for companies?

The most talked-about example of a CEO who must have startled awake boards and executives around the world is Elon Musk, who bought Twitter at the beginning of 2023 and immediately let a massive layoff storm sweep through the company. Tesla's shares plummeted... only to gently climb back up again, as has happened several times before. For the anonymous CEO, it was a victory. "You see! Nothing good comes from having such a celebrity CEO around." An executive who is bigger than the brand itself is often seen as a threat. There's always a moment when the genius seems just as much a fool. But it's also in such moments that you see the backbone of a CEO. How firmly do they stand? How do they deal with all those vocal opinions at that moment, criticising their every step?

A more positive example is Richard Branson, who also has the status of a celebrity CEO. When you talk about Branson in entrepreneurial circles, there's only one Branson, and that's Richard Branson.

The personal brand of a CEO has market value. But to whom does that market value belong? That is something that boards and investors do not always know how to handle. The real question is where the greatest risk really lies in 2023. Is it with a visible CEO or an invisible one? I hope I have provided an answer to that by now.

Human stories beat the corporate script

Following a thoughtful and validated script, filling your own social media channels with corporate news is comfortable and safe. And yet, research shows that in the leader's own voice and storytelling lies unparalleled power. Every contact, post, interview, or keynote is an opportunity to connect with customers, (future) employees, investors. And for every CEO who does not want to rule from an ivory tower, that's worth its weight in gold.

A beautiful example is Anouk Lagae, former CEO of Accent Jobs. I enjoyed guiding her through her keynote in which she 'dared' to weave elements from her personal life story into a message that transcends anecdotal storytelling. Anouk's mantra is "People first", and that's evident in everything she does. In what she radiates, says, and does. The former CEO of Accent Jobs is actively present on LinkedIn. Her profile reads "Views are my own". She happily hands out compliments, shares her views, points her readers to the insights and achievements of others. Her communication style is fluent; you can almost hear her through the words you read. Whether you see her speak on a stage, hear her on a podcast, or talk to her at a network event, Anouk is Anouk.

PODCAST ALERT
In my podcast, I had a conversation with **Anouk Lagae** about how she got to this point.

No 'one size fits all'

In the consideration of what you can or cannot communicate, there's also the how. And the how must match the leader's and the entrepreneur's style. It shouldn't sound fake or scripted, even if it's thoughtful and carefully considered.

What one CEO excels at may not be suited to another. Not every leader is extroverted, athletic, or a smooth talker. And that's okay. The most effective leaders are those who develop their own voice online and in real life, and do not simply copy and paste from colleagues they admire. The misunderstanding that prevents many leaders from becoming visible online leaders is the belief that they need to constantly send out positive and popular messages to the world. And preferably, to also throw their personal life into the mix. This is far from the truth. It can even backfire if there's no congruence with your personality.

You don't have to do it alone

My plea for top chiefs to be more visible and to dare to engage in an executive-personal branding process aligned with your company brand and employer brand does not mean you should be the only one. On the contrary. How strong would the company stand if the same happened with your team? Just as boards might be hesitant about a CEO who receives personal attention and becomes more famous than the brand, a CEO might have the same idea about employees. Executives and employees not being allowed to be visible online turns out to be the house policy more often than you think.

Why? Because the founder/CEO wants to be the only face. I know several companies where this is the case. Why is that? Because there's a fear their employees and executives might be headhunted. As if that chance isn't already a reality. And as if the decision to stay depends only on the employer. As if we still live and work in an economy where you want to work for the same employer for 40 years. So not the case. You should be happy if someone reaches five years of service.

At the Belgian company Protime, they're not afraid of letting people go. One of the first CEOs I coached was Peter s'Jongers. "People came, left after a few years, and then came back. Protime deals in time registration, so it's not a sexy product," Peter told me at the time. But employees liked identifying themselves online as #Protimers. An employer brand in action without marketing budgets. It's an example of a halo effect. The culture and personality of CEO Peter certainly played a part in that.

Why you should engage in personal branding as an employee

What if you're an employee? Should you also engage in personal branding? If you ask yourself this question while you're employed, your answer will probably be no. If you're unemployed, then it becomes yes. That seems to be the general trend observed on employees' profiles.

For most, LinkedIn is still just an online resume, nothing more, nothing less. After all, there's Facebook to share your life, and Instagram to collect your photo snapshots. Your job has nothing to do with it. Or does it? Because recruiters look for information about you to decide whether you'll be invited for an interview, I hope your Facebook doesn't show any compromising material. But starting to post while the green "Open to work" banner is on your LinkedIn profile is a bit like locking the stable door after the horse has bolted. It's like starting to bake a cake when your guests are already arriving.

Personal branding as a process should be a no-brainer today if you're not planning to spend your entire career with the same employer. You don't have to become a brand, a celebrity, or a thought leader (though you can if you want to) but making sure you lay a 'foundation' that allows HR and recruiters to get to know you without having to first meet you can already put you a step ahead of others.

But why not take your personal branding process a step further? As an employee, you can indeed become a personal brand without your employer seeing it as a threat. On the contrary, when you can and especially want to link your personal brand to the employer brand of your job, it's a win-win for both. It could even lead to a higher salary.

The American Miri Rodriguez is a brand consultant and senior storyteller at Microsoft. I met her on stage: me as a moderator and her as a speaker at UBA Trends Day. She creates a remarkable combination of her work at Microsoft and her personal brand. I find her approach to be quite refreshing and inspiring.

PODCAST ALERT

In my podcast, I have a conversation with **Miri Rodriguez** where she discusses how she was among the first at Microsoft to start personal branding, how she deals with AI, and how she draws the line between personal and private.

So, you're not doing it (just) for yourself

I hope I have been able to provide insight into why personal branding doesn't have to be an ego-driven process but can be a win-win story for you and your client/employer or investor. For me, the essence of personal branding is just as much about giving people the opportunity to get to know you in various ways, developing yourself into a personality with a strong vision in life and work, and also reflecting this outwardly.

Examining your deepest motivations, your reason for investing work, energy, and time in personal branding is an important and necessary exercise. Because for most professionals, it's not about fame per se, but what it can bring about: trust, credibility and, consequently, in a professional setting, economic growth.

And let me conclude this first part of the book by looking at personal branding purely from your perspective. So, not taking into account all the other players who could influence it.

Personal branding ***helps you to distinguish yourself from the competition***

In every industry, there are always other experts competing for the same attention and clients. With personal branding, you help clients to see the difference between experts offering similar services more clearly and to remember you.

Personal branding ***makes you more credible***

When people see you as an authority in your field, they are more likely to collaborate with you. This way, people are more inclined to believe in your capabilities and trust your advice. But remember: if you want people to take your expertise seriously, you must ensure that your personal brand is credible. Fake it till you make it is not the path you want to take.

Personal branding ***gives you confidence***

A strong personal brand is like wearing clothes in which you feel beautiful and strong. It provides you with a guide on what to do and what not to do. You will be less insecure during networking and self-promotion. It's how you want people to see you, and it's a big part of the reason why they choose to work with you or not. Customers want to connect with personal brands and brands that make them feel good and inspired. Having or being a personal brand is thus a win-win for both you and your client.

Personal branding helps you ***build your legacy***

But the most beautiful advantage that personal branding can offer is often discovered by most professionals only in the later stages of their career. Personal branding allows you to change course during your career and to connect your entire career as a body of work. In other words, thanks to personal branding, you can work on a magnum opus.

Summary of Chapter 3: Personal branding as a growth marketing strategy

8 things to remember:

1. You need to know why you want to get into personal branding. If you don't, you will not be able to sustain your efforts.
2. The why is different for a solopreneur, employee or executive.
3. Aligning your personal brand with the company brand shows how committed you are.
4. Aligning your personal brand with the employer brand builds trust with employees and potential candidates.
5. Personal branding is about you, but not only about you.
6. Personal branding impacts your clients, your investors and employees in a good way too.
7. People want to know who they work for, work with or buy from.
8. Your personal brand is what you make of it.

Chapter 4: Own your journey

Your life, your work, your journey

Personal branding is always associated with building fame and authority in what you do at that stage of your life. It's usually perceived and viewed as a marketing strategy aimed at acquiring more of something.

But what if you see it as a foundation for your 'body of work', your 'oeuvre', your 'intellectual legacy'? That's when it becomes truly interesting. After all, there comes a time in everyone's life when they decide to tackle things differently. But just like a snake shedding its skin, you remain you. Just as a caterpillar in its cocoon becomes a butterfly, it remains the same creature. Therefore, I believe it's very important that the foundation is correct.

When I was a child, I saw how my young parents worked themselves to the bone in the wholesale business they had been obliged to take over from my grandfather. Both my mother and father were pulled out of school by their parents at the age of 15 to work in the family business. On my mother's side, they were farmers, and on my father's side, wholesalers of fruit and vegetables. The two teenagers met at the wholesale market in Brussels where they were engaged several nights a week as free labour. During the day, my mother worked in the fields, did the bookkeeping and the household chores. My father delivered goods to retailers and washed tons of carrots. The other children in the family were allowed to go to school and pursued further studies. That's how it was in those days, apparently.

My mother was a wise and entrepreneurial girl who didn't get the chance to develop herself further. My father had a talent for drawing and was a good athlete, two talents he pursued further only after his retirement. My mother was unlucky; she had her first stroke at 29, and more would follow that would forever change her path in life. From the age of twelve, I helped in the business, did household chores, and took care of my mother when she had to go to the hospital or was recovering. During school holidays, my younger brother and I accompanied our parents to work at the wholesale market in Brussels at night. But, unlike them, I did go to school, followed dancing and acting classes, and finished high school.

I must have felt the effect of missed opportunities and suppressed dreams, because I clearly remember asking myself as a young girl: what do you want to be able to say about your life when you're dying? And my answer was – and still is – that I have utilised the talents I possess, big or small, to their fullest. That I wouldn't wait until my retirement to do the things I enjoy. The young ianka made that promise to herself, and looking back at my path now, that is also the path I have followed. It is the path of what I later learned to be a Renaissance person.

> According to Britannica, the Renaissance man, also called the universal person, the Italian uomo universale, is an ideal that developed in Renaissance Italy by Leon Battista Alberti (1404–72), stating that "A person can do all things if they will." The ideal embodied the basic principles of Renaissance humanism, which regarded humans as limitless in their capacity for development, and led to the idea that people should strive to embrace all knowledge and develop their own abilities as fully as possible. The most famous uomo universale is Leonardo da Vinci (1452–1519).

The result was that I often did not conform to the prevailing norms in my field at the time.

My urge to explore, rebel, learn, adopt, and build my life's work led to a whole list of job descriptions when I introduced myself. I was an actor,

What do you want to be able to say about your life when you're on your deathbed?

writer, director, radio presenter, TV presenter, publisher. I was passionate about understanding the human condition and tried to capture and translate it into various forms of storytelling. However, because people think in terms of job functions and chronologically ordered CVs, they interpreted this as a sign of indecisiveness, lack of focus, lack of work. They were confused because I was simultaneously successful. What they didn't see was the common thread of storytelling and the role of questioning that connected everything for me. After all, it wasn't the descriptions that defined my work; those were just words attached to functions, to skills. Skills that I could use to create my larger story. It was about what I could achieve with them.

For those now tempted to label me as a 'creative generalist', then also add highly gifted, autistic, ADHD, blue, yellow, red, green, expert, perfectionist, non-conformist, highly sensitive, stoic, maverick, explorer, sage. I embody elements of each label or type. Ask yourself why you are so stuck on labels.

While people hop from job to job, from company to company, from project to project, building a linear CV that they post on LinkedIn like a timeline, I believe in creating a narrative, where everything you do contributes to your body of work, your oeuvre. And although the term 'oeuvre' is traditionally associated with the body of work of an artist or writer (which I still am at heart as a storyteller), I want to introduce the concept as a richer way to approach your career and personal branding.

The artist and his oeuvre

In the life of an artist, an oeuvre refers to the collection of work they have created over the course of their career. It showcases their creative journey through changing styles, exploring different themes, and developing skills over a long period. An oeuvre offers a holistic view of their total work. A prime example of this is the work of Pablo Picasso. His oeuvre spans more than seven decades and illustrates a continuous evolution of style and technique – from the Blue Period, the Rose Period, the African art-inspired period to Cubism. All these different styles from each period contribute to a holistic view of Picasso's extensive oeuvre.

In the body of work of an artist, we can also discover a 'magnum opus'. This is that one masterpiece or a collection of masterpieces that best reflects or encapsulates their skills, innovative thought, and the summation of their contribution to their art form. The magnum opus is often seen as the work with which the artist is most associated and that has had a significant and lasting impact on their field.

In the work of Picasso, who was also known as a womaniser and made women his muses, *Les Demoiselles d'Avignon* is considered his magnum opus. This painting marked a radical break from traditional European painting and led to the emergence of Cubism, a revolutionary style co-founded by Picasso himself. The work not only showcases Picasso's innovative artistic techniques but also encapsulates his courage to defy norms and push boundaries.

Beethoven's Ninth Symphony, especially its final movement, 'Ode to Joy', is often regarded as his magnum opus. The Ninth Symphony was groundbreaking as it was the first time a major composer used voices in a symphony. Schiller's poem 'Ode to Joy' was set to music by Beethoven and sung by a choir. And this while the man was nearly deaf when he composed the symphony. Did you know that the work was chosen as the European anthem by the Council of Europe in 1972?

These two concepts – the oeuvre and the magnum opus – offer us a fascinating glimpse into the career of an artist. The life's work allows us to gain a panoramic view of how an artist has grown, experimented, and developed in their craft. The magnum opus, on the other hand, shows us both a pinnacle and a reflection of the artist's identity, growth, and impact.

The professional and his oeuvre

When you hear the term 'oeuvre', you automatically think of artists or writers, individuals who produce tangible pieces of artistic work. But what if you applied this concept in a broader professional context? What if you considered the entire body of work you have produced over a career – whether it be in business, academia, technology, or other fields – as a 'professional oeuvre'?

Don't get me wrong, I'm not placing artistic oeuvre and professional oeuvre in opposition as amateurish versus professional. By professional, I mean to encompass a collection of academic, technological, intellectual, and business oeuvres.

A professional oeuvre could consist of projects you've led, products you've developed, services you've delivered, ideas you've introduced, or changes you've implemented. Just like an artist's oeuvre, your professional oeuvre showcases your journey, your growth, and your contribution to your field.

But isn't that just your resumé? you might think. A traditional CV, or curriculum vitae, as you might also see on your LinkedIn profile, provides a linear, chronological overview of your professional journey, often starting with your education, followed by your work experience, and then your skills and references. The primary focus of a CV is on your formal qualifications, job titles, and the roles you've played in various positions. It doesn't capture the essence of your professional identity. It's a list of names and cryptic business descriptions, not your unique approach to problem-solving, the initiative you take, the impact of your work, or the soft skills you've developed. It doesn't show your professional growth or the breadth and depth of your experiences. While a CV can tell a potential employer where you've worked and what roles you've held, it doesn't necessarily show what you're capable of, what you've achieved, or who you are as a professional.

Changing your understanding of professional achievements

Instead of viewing your career as a series of jobs or roles, you start to see it as a cohesive body of work which you contribute to, refine, and expand throughout your professional life. As a journey filled with experiences. It's a holistic representation of your career. It encourages you to think beyond job titles and roles and instead focus on what you've created, which problems you've solved, which changes you've implemented, and what impact you've had. It also encourages you to not see your career as a linear path but as an ongoing process of creation, much like the work of an artist. It shifts your focus from climbing the career ladder to creating meaningful, impactful life's work. This may even lead you to make different career choices. In other words, the traditional CV does not help you showcase the significance and growth characteristic of an oeuvre. You need to start looking differently at how you can present your work as an oeuvre. And you do this, just like artists, by compiling or curating a portfolio.

Curate your work as a portfolio

Presenting your career as a portfolio offers a more comprehensive and nuanced view of your professional life. A portfolio can include a variety of items: reports you've written, projects you've led, case studies you've developed, presentations you've given, or innovative solutions you've implemented. Work that you document with personal branding tactics that I describe later in this book.

A portfolio captures the essence of your career in a way a CV cannot. It shows not only the positions you've held but also the work you've done and the results you've achieved. For example, it illustrates your problem-solving skills, creativity, leadership qualities, and capacity for innovation.

A portfolio also shows your professional growth over time. By including work from different stages of your career, you can show how your skills have evolved, how your thinking has matured, and how your understanding of your field has deepened.

Additionally, a portfolio will reflect your personal brand – your unique combination of skills, experiences, values, and personality traits. This is particularly important in today's competitive job market, where employers are looking for individuals who stand out and bring something unique to the table.

> Albert Einstein is widely regarded as one of the most influential physicists in history, and his theory of relativity is often considered his magnum opus. This theory, which includes the famous equation $E=mc^2$, revolutionised how we understand the fundamental laws of the universe. Einstein's work on the theory of relativity introduced concepts such as the curvature of spacetime and the equivalence of energy and mass, fundamentally changing our understanding of gravity and the interrelation of space and time. The theory still shapes how we study physics and cosmology today, demonstrating its lasting impact. In addition to his specific scientific contributions, Einstein's curious nature, perseverance, and dedication to understanding the universe's mysteries all contributed to his personal brand and legacy as a scientist. Einstein's theory of relativity is not just his most significant scientific achievement or his magnum opus but also a reflection of his unique approach to science and his enduring influence on our understanding of the universe. His example shows how a scientist's magnum opus can be a body of work or a major theory that advances knowledge in his field and leaves a lasting legacy.

PODCAST ALERT
Listen to the conversations I have with artists and curators of exhibitions.

Creating your professional oeuvre: a step-by-step guide

Creating a portfolio that makes your professional oeuvre visible requires careful consideration, planning, and execution. Here are the steps:

Step 1: Identify key projects and achievements
Begin by listing the most meaningful moments, projects, and achievements of your career. This could range from a product you developed, a project you coordinated, a campaign you designed, a process you improved, or a problem you solved. Record everything that had a significant impact, where your contribution was crucial, or that you're exceptionally proud of. Don't be swayed by just including the most prestigious names and titles. Consider the personal and professional value it brought.

Step 2: Uncover skills and growth
Next, reflect on the skills each part of your portfolio demonstrates. This includes both hard skills – specific, teachable abilities relevant to a particular job – and soft skills such as communication, teamwork, or problem-solving. Also, include pieces from different stages of your career to show your professional development over time. Dig deep enough in your exploration. For example, 'communication' is quite general and vague. There are elements of communication where you're less strong, and others where you excel. Look for those specific elements, as they have shaped you into who you are.

Step 3: Highlight innovation and impact
In each portfolio item, highlight where you introduced innovative ideas or approaches, showcasing your innovative thinking. Furthermore, quantify the impact of your work where possible. Did it increase revenue, improve efficiency, enhance customer satisfaction, or deliver another measurable result? Concrete evidence of your impact enhances the value of each item. Think deeply about this. Small, inconspicuous steps might have had a butterfly effect in your life that you're unaware of. This is also the case with painters.

Step 4: Align your portfolio with your professional goals

Ensure that your portfolio aligns with your future career goals and effectively represents your personal brand. If you're an innovator, your portfolio should reflect that. If you're a master organiser, include work that showcases this skill. Ensure the work you select and the way you present it matches how you want others to see you professionally.

Not all skills on your resume are worth highlighting for you personally. You want to move forward, not be held back by skills you might be good at but that don't propel you forward.

Step 5: Make your oeuvre visible

A painter, visual artist, or photographer sets up an exhibition. A catalogue is created with a foreword discussing the artist's impact and an interview with the artist to hear their story. How will you showcase your oeuvre? On an 'about me' page, a book, a video, ...

Remember: Creating your professional oeuvre is an ongoing process that will evolve as your career progresses. This guide offers a starting point, but don't forget to continually update and refine your portfolio as you take on new projects and roles and acquire new skills. And the fun part is, if you want to make a career switch, you can perfectly incorporate it into your oeuvre because you've built it on personal and professional development, not on job functions.

Summary of Chapter 4: Own your journey

5 things to remember:

1. Stop showing your professional career as a CV.
2. Start experiencing and presenting your career like an artist's oeuvre.
3. Curate your work as a portfolio instead of a list of jobs.
4. Define your magnum opus. Yes, you have one!
5. Follow the step-by-step guide in creating your professional oeuvre.

PART 3: PERSONAL(ITY)

Chapter 5: From personal to personality

Your professional oeuvre takes us on a tour of your key projects, accomplishments, and experiences that reflect your unique skills, style, and impact. It's not merely a summary of what you've done, but also an in-depth reflection on how and why you've done it and continue to do so. And perhaps you've already realised this, but the work that encapsulates the essence of this entire journey and encompasses everything is you. And when you set out to turn that work into a masterpiece that everyone can see, your magnum opus, then you're working on what I call your personality brand. Your portfolio is your unique opportunity to strengthen your personality brand, provided you use it correctly. That's why I want to emphasise that it's essential to provide context for the work you've done throughout your career. Stay true to yourself and showcase projects that align with your values, ambitions, and passions. Let your portfolio map out your professional journey, with successes and obstacles, like a story. Highlight what sets you apart. Show where you truly make a difference. And continue to develop yourself, for an oeuvre is never complete.

The traditional path – understanding conventional personal branding

The typical approach to personal branding can be encapsulated in one term: marketing. It's about forging a polished, marketable and, above all, static self-image to present to the world. It revolves around brand recognition, followers, data, and algorithms. This is not inherently incorrect, but it only illustrates a part of the bigger picture.

These are the most common steps:

Self-reflection: Here, you identify your competencies, passions, and values. What are you good at? What do you enjoy doing? Which beliefs guide your actions? What are your weaknesses? These are some of the questions that, according to the traditional approach, you need to explore.

Formulating your **Unique Selling Proposition (USP)**: The focus here is on determining what sets your product/service apart from your competitors and how it can lead to more sales. Your personality can be a part of this.

Identifying and reaching your **target audience**: In the traditional approach, great emphasis is placed on identifying who needs to know about you and your USP. I see this as a pitfall. Because who chooses whom? And why? You may have a certain ideal audience in mind, but reality will show whether your personality really suits them and whether your level of knowledge matches theirs. Or will you pretend to be someone else? Who are truly the people who will benefit most from what you have to offer?

And then there's the creation of your **personal brand statement**, a concise declaration that summarises your USP and your value. It's what you want people to associate with your name and usually relates to what you want to sell. Your elevator pitch. Unfortunately, for most people, it sounds the same and they all seem like saints. "I help ambitious entrepreneurs discover their strength and enhance their mindset so they stand stronger in their leadership."

And finally: Creating and managing **your online presence**: Here, the emphasis is on creating a consistent image across various platforms. This includes maintaining a professional presence on social media, sharing content relevant to your brand, and regularly updating your profile on professional networking sites like LinkedIn. It's mostly about data and analytics, pleasing algorithms, and engaging with hot topic trends.

The oeuvre approach – why it's smarter than traditional personal branding

The traditional approach often focuses on creating an image, while the oeuvre approach is about creating a real, consistent, but evolving identity. An identity that from its creation is full of stories and emotion, two elements that people who want to get to know you love.

You're not forced to create a persona. It is an option. Because with each job, you build towards an improved version of yourself. You're part of something bigger. This can build stronger relationships and more trust with your audience. You'll also find it easier to establish consistency based on your integrity and personality. This results in personal branding that remains consistent over time and, especially, across different contexts, which is much more credible and compelling. An oeuvre is a long-term effort, and by working on it, you accept that. Your personal branding process will also gain more depth. After all, it's not just about what you can do, but also about who you are, what you've learned, how you've grown, and what you stand for. This depth can make your brand more accessible and inspiring. You don't become a personal brand but a personality brand.

You develop resilience. By basing your personality branding on working on an oeuvre, you create a brand that withstands changes. Industries evolve, job roles change, but your core – your personality, values, and experiences – remains. This means that in your personal branding process, you remain relevant and powerful, regardless of the changes that come your way. Ultimately, working on an oeuvre is about creating a legacy, not just a brand. It's about the lasting impact you make in your field. It's not just about what you do, but also how you do it, why you do it, and for whom you do it. This legacy will continue to inspire others, even after you have moved on.

In short, by viewing your work as the oeuvre of an artist, I want you to go beyond just selling the product (yourself). The focus is on creating a masterpiece that tells a story (your journey). It's a continuous process of self-discovery, growth, and expression, leading to a personality brand that is not only compelling but also sustainable and truly yours. And by doing this, you work on your magnum opus, that one work in the oeuvre that is all-encompassing and tells the best, the essence of the artist (you).

Own your story

"Own your story. Or someone else will." The title of this book is not just a catchy, somewhat scratchy sentence. It's a mantra, a call to action, a challenge. It reminds you that if you don't actively create and share your story, others will fill the vacuum, often with inaccuracies or falsehoods.

Your magnum opus and your oeuvre are essentially your story – a story crafted by your hands, shaped by your personality, and brought to life through your experiences. It's a story that goes beyond a list of achievements or a neatly packaged brand. It delves deeper into your growth, your resilience, your values, and your vision. It showcases your unique personality – your strengths, your quirks, your passions.

When you own that story, you also have control. You define the consistent elements for which you want to be known. You celebrate your journey, with all its ups and downs. You decide for yourself how you want to be seen, rather than leaving it up to the assumptions or prejudices of others. That's why I love this approach so much. It transcends hype, trends, algorithms. It enables you to create a personality brand and thought leadership that's not about an image, but about an identity. Not just about a product or knowledge, but about a person. It helps you create a legacy that is authentic and unequivocally you.

Ultimately, personality branding is not just about what you want to achieve. It's about who you want to be and how you want to be remembered. It's about your place in the world, your impact on others, and the footprints you leave behind. It's about your magnum opus.

So, embrace your unique palette. Paint with bold strokes. Create your masterpiece. Own your story, or someone else will. The canvas is wide, the colours are vibrant, and the world is waiting for the best version of you. And let's start with that today.

But beware! Although creating a magnum opus and achieving success are related, they are not the same. Success is often measured in tangible terms: wealth, recognition, professional achievements, and so on. It is usually defined by external indicators and is often subject to societal norms and expectations. What is considered successful in one culture or industry may not be considered so in another culture or industry.

On the other hand, a magnum opus refers to an individual's most significant work or contribution in their field. It's a reflection of their values, their unique skills and talents, and their impact. It doesn't always lead to traditional markers of success such as wealth or fame. Some artists and thinkers were not recognised during their lifetime, and their work was only appreciated posthumously as a magnum opus.

But a magnum opus often leads to a different kind of success, a success that is more profound and lasting: the success of creating something meaningful, of influencing others, of leaving a legacy. It represents a journey of self-discovery, a dedication to one's craft, and a contribution that makes an indelible mark on one's field. With this, I want to convey that you can see and approach your personal branding and thought leadership as a marketing strategy, but also as a part or the culmination of your life's work. I hope this book will inspire you to work on both.

> Elon Musk really doesn't need to worry about personal branding. It probably doesn't even interest him. And why should it? His actions speak volumes. He has quickly moved to an oeuvre way of thinking. Musk, a polymath among entrepreneurs, has a vision that spans across various sectors such as electric cars (Tesla), space exploration (SpaceX), and neurotechnology (Neuralink), just to name a few. While each is

notably innovative on its own, many people consider SpaceX his magnum opus, thinking about the idea of making human life multi-planetary. His bold dreams, willingness to take risks, and relentless drive have shaped his personality brand. He is known for setting and pursuing challenging goals, whether it's revolutionising transport on Earth or colonising Mars. His magnum opus is thus not limited to one venture or project, but is manifested in his constant pursuit of groundbreaking innovation across various industries.

The early bird's advantage

In this book, I address professionals with a reputation, which essentially means they have a track record of ten years under their belt. But to claim that building an oeuvre and a magnum opus requires a lifetime of work is akin to saying that an artist can only create their masterpiece after decades of work.

It's not an endgame – it's a journey that starts the moment you begin your career or start your business. It's about a mindset. How you approach your story, work, and life. That's how I've always done it.

Starting early gives you an advantage. From the beginning, you'll learn to understand yourself better – your values, your passions, your strengths, and areas where you need to grow. This can guide your career or business decisions, making them more aligned with your authentic self.

By becoming aware of recurring elements that seem to bear your signature, you can weave them into your work from the beginning. This way, over time, you build a strong, consistent personality brand. But beware: don't get too attached. Grow and evolve.

If you're a millennial or Gen Z, then you might have been documenting your growth journey from the start by being on social media. But are you doing this consciously, or are you showing just about everything in your life? If approached wisely, this can be a rich source to learn from, reflect upon, and draw inspiration, both for yourself and others. Look at the American entrepreneur, investor, and internet personality Gary Vaynerchuk. People start forming an image of you from the moment they discover you. By working on your personal brand early on, you can influence these perceptions to align with your authentic self. As a result, you attract people who resonate with your values and vision. These can become lifelong professional relationships that enrich your career or business.

The world and work are constantly in motion. With a well-defined personal brand, you are better equipped to withstand these changes while remaining flexible. Every step you take, every decision you make, every project you undertake contributes to your legacy. Starting early gives you a head start in building this legacy.

Your magnum opus is a living, evolving body of work. Every day brings new experiences, new lessons, and new achievements – all things that add a stroke to your masterpiece. So don't wait for the 'right' moment. Pick up your brush now and start painting your personal brand. The canvas is wide, and the palette is entirely yours.

Summary of Chapter 5: From personal to personality

6 things to remember:

1. Personal branding uses the same strategy as company branding.
2. Personal branding is static.
3. Presenting your work as an oeuvre opens the mind to an evolving career.
4. Personality branding grows with your personality.
5. Personality branding is flux.
6. Start to own your story.

Lannoo
Campus

Chapter 6: How's your personality doing?

I believe that by working on an oeuvre and embracing the freedom of exploration and growth within it, you are also working on and shaping your personality.

You'll often hear me say that I think personal branding needs rebranding. And I truly mean that. Just because something is personal doesn't necessarily mean it has personality. That's why the cover of this book features the words 'personality branding', which is a combination of personal + personality + branding. I advocate for more personality in personal branding and less focus on the marketing side.

Perhaps you've already sensed it in the previous chapter, but the role of developing personality is crucial when you want to become a personal brand or thought leader. But what do I mean by personality? Let me attempt to explain by taking you cross-industry, to the world of acting.

Creating personality on command

The creation of a personality

While as a human you shape your personality by living your life, an actor consciously creates personalities for a living. Let me take you through that process.

When I, as an actor, accepted a new role, I received the screenplay, script, or play by mail. Reading a script is not like reading a novel. You only have dialogues between characters at your disposal. Situations are divided into episodes and scenes. For each scene, you get a very brief description of what the environment looks like, and you read about the actions taking place. So, you read pages of conversations between people, supplemented with a minimum of information describing accompanying actions.

From these conversations, you start to create the personality. It's incredible how much you can learn about someone's personality through their use of words, sentence construction, reactions, punctuation, and actions, even reading 'between the lines'. Then, as an actor, you work on congruence between the interpretation of the text and emotions, translated into body language, sound, and movement.

Congruence is the key to authenticity

The greatest and at the same time strangest compliment on my work as an actor was when people could not see or feel the distinction between me and my character. I was experienced as authentic while, as a 21-year-old, playing a 16-year-old girl in the theatre. To this day, people who once saw me portray the whimsical Princess Prieeltje expect my personality to be similar. In almost every interview, there's an inquiry into how your character resembles you. Even though everyone knows you're acting, the boundary often seems blurred.

As an actor, you learn to be congruent in portraying your character. You constantly think about "How would my character react to this? How do they move in this situation?" You pause to consider the options and choose the one that fits best. Either you feel for yourself whether something works or not, or your colleagues point out that it's not credible. The more congruent, the more credible.

As an actor, by consistently working with congruence, you also notice when someone is not congruent and is completely unaware of it. That's why I'm wary when people want to take courses in body language – while the insights are valid, the execution doesn't achieve the desired result.

The reason is often that the focus is on one element of body language, while an interpretation is the result of a combination of signals. When body language is not aligned with the person's thinking, feeling, and speaking, it still doesn't feel authentic, because the congruence is missing.

Your sticky factor, your Velcro

Just like a film, song, or theatre script can have remakes where the story remains the same but yields a different result, the development of personalities can too.

A screenwriter has a certain envisioning of the character in mind when writing and tries to convey that in the script. Once the script is in the hands of a director, they too will give it their own interpretation. After all, there are different ways to shape the drama between Romeo and Juliet, for example, even though the story remains the same.

Being cast for the role as an actor means, on one hand, that you fit the director's interpretation best. On the other hand, it's expected that you, as an actor, will also make it your own. And once you start working with your co-actor, you see that the impact of what he or she does with their role also influences your interpretation of the character. Actually, you deal with different perceptions of the same personality. If the script is rock solid, then discussions are kept to a minimum. If not, interpretations can vary widely, and discussions will ensue about the final choice to be used. This is simply because each production – whether it's film, television, or theatre – has a specific goal or result that it works towards.

What effect do we aim to achieve, what impression or impact do we want to make? And which aspects of a personality are we going to highlight the most in the characters? You'll investigate which emphases you'll place on which character traits of the character, which you'll accentuate to get your story told better and which others not.

As an individual, you continually make choices about what aspects of your personality to show, where to show them, and to what extent. Context, environment, and emotions play a big role in this. Perceptions of what is and isn't acceptable, social codes, may lead you to have learned to suppress certain aspects of your personality and not others.

You behave somewhat differently at work than at home with your friends; you share different things about yourself in intimate circles compared to during a job interview. A person wears different hats, has different roles to fulfil, and the difference in behaviour can be large or small. You'll show certain aspects of your personality more or less depending on the situation you're in or the goal you have in mind.

When you aim to score high in personal branding, this is where the differentiator lies. On one hand, you'll need to become aware of the aspects of your personality that can ensure you make more impact and have more influence. On the other hand, you'll also need to be willing to employ these more, and perhaps even exaggerate them. And that can go against some codes, rules, habits.

Two trends: persona versus authenticity

Authenticity is seen today as a sacred cow that you're not supposed to challenge, but what I notice is that it's often used as an excuse and a cover up. Authenticity has become a commodity. There's a difference between being authentic, being perceived as authentic, or presenting oneself as authentic.

- People who are authentic generally don't concern themselves with how they come across to others. They don't even think about it. And then, in the personal branding process, it can go two ways. Either they disappear into the crowd when it turns out they have no added value for others. Or they get noticed for their achievements, and their authenticity contributes to their personal branding. Once this becomes clear to them, they will start to use and maintain this more consciously because it also benefits them. And then it's a matter of waiting to see how long it remains credibly authentic.

- Being perceived as authentic is what happens most often. It means you've found a tribe that resonates with what you think and feel and identifies with you. To them, you are authentic; to others, you're not. If you've found such a tribe, it's important to discover why you resonate with them. They have chosen you, not the other way around. As a result, if you decide to change, they might not want to follow you anymore.

- Presenting oneself as authentic is the reality for many. In your quest to find out who you are and who you want to be, you realise there's still unexplored territory in your personality. The moment you think, "This is really me and I've always suppressed it, but now I'm just going to show it," you use that as an excuse to show your new identity immediately instead of becoming it. Then you get the "Fake it till you make it" syndrome, where people suddenly appear overconfident, extroverted, loud, and ambitious. They are authentic in their desire but not in their expression.

I want to make it clear that in your professional life and your work, there's always a point where you cultivate your authenticity and work with a persona. Even if only because in every role you play, you carry a different responsibility and want to send a certain image of yourself into the world.

Such a persona can be based on certain aspects of your personality but is usually enhanced or even slightly different from your authentic self. This approach is often used in sectors where a strong, distinctive personality can help you stand out. And that's all okay, as long as you can handle it, it doesn't happen too abruptly, it's credible, and you enjoy it. Developing congruence in your thinking, feeling, and doing takes time.

> For example, Steve Jobs, the late co-founder of Apple, had a personality that was visionary and perfectionist. This personality, complete with his signature black turtleneck and jeans, helped to strengthen the narrative of Jobs as a unique innovator and established a distinctive personal brand. Just remember that a persona, to be successful and sustainable, must have some grounding in your true self. It shouldn't be a façade, or you risk it not being credible.

Personal branding is not always about creating a larger-than-life persona or being the most charismatic person in the room. It's about credibility and consistently showing your personality and what makes you unique.

Here are a few examples of individuals with strong personal brands known for their understated or reserved personality:

> Warren Buffett: Known as 'the Oracle of Omaha', Buffett's personal brand is tied to his reputation as a wise and successful investor. He's not flashy or charismatic as many might expect of a billionaire. Instead, his brand is built on his profound knowledge of finance, his disciplined investment strategy, and his down-to-earth, humane charm. He's known for his integrity, humility, and commitment to philanthropy, all of which contribute to a personal brand that's respected in the financial world.

> Angela Merkel: As Chancellor of Germany from 2005 to 2021, Merkel was known for her pragmatic and analytical approach to leadership. Her personal brand was not built on charisma or personal magnetism but on her reputation as a stable and reliable leader. Known as 'Mutti' (mother) in Germany, her brand is associated with her rational decision-making, commitment to European unity, and ability to navigate complex political issues.

> Tim Cook: As the CEO of Apple, Cook had big shoes to fill following the death of Steve Jobs, who had a strong, charismatic personal brand. However, Cook has created his own personal brand that stands on its own. He is known for his operational genius, commitment to the environment, and advocacy for privacy and human rights. While less charismatic and visionary than Jobs, his personal brand is built on his ability to lead one of the world's most valuable companies while upholding his personal values.

Each of these individuals is respected and influential in their fields. These examples show that a personal brand can be built on work, expertise, and values, rather than on a flashy personality.

Toward four criteria to strengthen personality

Personality is an individual characteristic way of thinking, feeling, and behaving. It refers to the enduring characteristics and behaviours that have shaped a person's unique adaptation to life, including interests, motivations, values, self-image, abilities, and emotional patterns.

At the beginning of a personal branding process, most professionals don't focus on leveraging their personality. They primarily focus on sharing their expertise online and showing what they can do. This is evident in the amount of how-to content they share, the numerous tips they give away for free. In this way, they aim to position themselves in the market as experts. This approach can create a large online following and even the necessary fame that brings them to stages as speakers. What you notice next is that these experts also start working on developing, accentuating, and communicating other aspects and tactics in personal branding.

If you now think back to the chapter where I introduced the concept of oeuvre thinking and working on a magnum opus as a metaphor for your personal brand, where would you place the just-described step in personal branding? As a work in your oeuvre? Or as the start of your magnum opus? It's the former: a work in your oeuvre. Sharing your expertise is just that, sharing what you can do. And what you can do, others can do too. Unless you add your personality to it and thereby demonstrate a clear difference.

What an actor must explore to create a character is comparable to the work you can do to become aware of your personality. All the information is within you; unlocking it and examining what you can do with it to make your personality more visible and impactful to achieve your goal is your task. If you were to break down the work into criteria by which you can measure the impact of a personality, for me, it would be substance, style, conviction, and unfair advantage. The higher you climb on the ladder in personal branding, the more you need to distinguish yourself in these areas.

If you work on these four criteria you will add more value to the knowledge you have and want to sell. The ultimate goal is to achieve congruence between the four criteria and your knowledge.

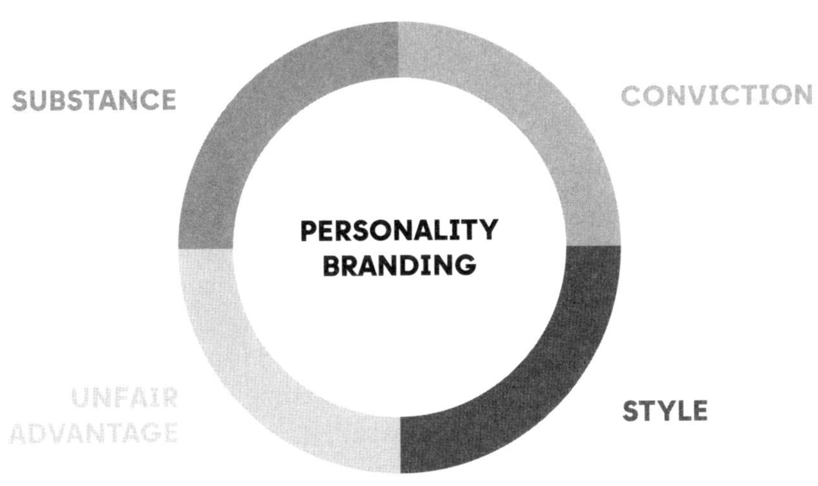

The four criteria that strengthen your personality brand. The stronger and more outspoken they are, the bigger your personality brand becomes.

Substance

Let's start with the most challenging one, substance. The higher up the ladder of personal branding in a business context, the more 'substance' is expected of you. But substance should not be confused with mere knowledge and experience.

'Knowledge' refers to the understanding, facts, information that someone has acquired through learning and education. It includes knowledge about a subject or field, understanding its principles, and being aware of various concepts and theories. Experience or expertise indicates a level of skill, competence, and mastery in a specific area. Experts have extensive experience, practical know-how, and the ability to effectively apply their knowledge to solve complex problems or excel in their domain.

When building a personal brand, it's essential to highlight your education, training, skills, and professional experience to position yourself as an authority or specialist in your field. Demonstrating your expertise can make your audience see you as someone with knowledge and proficiency, which can build trust and credibility around your personal brand.

But with knowledge and expertise alone, you will not distinguish yourself from others anymore. That was possible in the pre-internet era because information was not accessible. Today, anyone with an internet connection can gain knowledge, and subsequently, experience and expertise. Sharing knowledge and expertise is still the first step in personal branding to make yourself visible. After all, there are always people looking for what you know and they do not, and who want a shortcut. You then offer that shortcut by sharing your knowledge. This happens on a massive scale, and what you see is that some manage to grow a very large following and gain corresponding fame as a result. They become, what I will later call in this book, a trusted expert and balance between the first level 'visible expert' and the second level 'personal brand' in the personal branding process. Then comes a point where they need to work on substance. If they don't, they remain in the social media friend zone.

While knowledge and expertise are important components of personal branding, they are not sufficient on their own to create a personality that advances your branding. Substance does that. While knowledge and expertise can contribute to substance, the term refers to the inherent value and significance of something or someone beyond experience and information.

The key to moving from mere knowledge sharing and expertise to substance is developing a Unique Point of View (UPOV). A UPOV represents your own perspective, insights, and approach to a specific topic or industry. It's the lens through which you view the world and share your knowledge and expertise, distinguishing you from others in your field.

This is what a Unique Point of View (UPOV) can bring you in strengthening your personality, building your substance, and ultimately your personal branding:

- **Differentiation:** A UPOV allows you to stand out from your competitors. In a crowded market, showcasing a fresh and distinctive perspective can capture your target audience's attention and make you stand out.

- **Thought leadership:** The stronger and more expansive your UPOV becomes, the better the chance you can position yourself as a thought leader in your industry.

- **Strength:** Developing and sharing a unique perspective requires congruence and the courage to express your true beliefs and ideas. By embracing your unique perspective, you can be genuine and relatable, which resonates with your audience.

- **Value proposition**: A unique viewpoint is part of your value proposition. It becomes a compelling reason for the audience to pay attention to you and engage with your content, products, or services.

- **Content creation:** A unique viewpoint fuels content creation. It provides a consistent theme and direction, aligning with your brand and resonating with your target audience.

By embracing a unique perspective, you can develop substance, enhance the content of your personal brand, and have a lasting impact on your audience. It allows you to bring forth your personality and share valuable insights that capture the attention and loyalty of your followers. Developing and articulating a UPOV is a continuous process that requires ongoing self-reflection, learning, and refining of ideas.

It's not always easy to develop one, so let me give you an example.

Not your Barbie girl in a Barbie world

As I write this chapter, Barbie Mania reigns, and the movie has broken the Warner Bros Box Office record in its opening week. I was disappointed when I first saw the photos of Margot Robbie and Ryan Gosling as Barbie and Ken on social media. I didn't understand why such good actors were tempted to act in *Barbie*, the movie, and why Robbie wanted to produce the film. Now that the marketing machine is in full swing, Margot Robbie is seen in every Barbie outfit available, and it seems like a giant pot of pink paint has been thrown over the world. I wonder why everyone is so crazy about it. I don't see its relevance. I fear for the mental health of hundreds of thousands of viewers. However, it was something the actress said in one of her interviews about the origin story of Barbie that made me decide to buy a ticket to see the movie.

> Ruth Handler, the co-founder of Mattel, revolutionised the toy industry when she invented a doll that looked like an adult woman. Before Barbie, girls mostly played with baby dolls, which conditioned them to become mothers. In the early

1950s, Handler had the rather revolutionary idea that playing with dolls modelled after adult women (with breasts – ooh la la...) would help girls imagine what they could become when they grew up. And in Ruth's world, anything was possible: mechanic, accountant, movie star, hairdresser, boss, ... Handler was inspired by her daughter Barbara, after whom she would name her iconic doll Barbie. Ruth Handler had a Unique Point of View (UPOV) on dolls and how they could influence the lives of girls.

Thirty years later, when I played with Barbies in the early '80s, I was annoyed by the ideal image they imposed on me: to be beautiful, you had to be blonde, have large breasts, a slim waist, and long legs. Ruth's 'purpose' was no longer needed; the perception of women had shifted to another ideal.

In 2023, I wonder why they are still on the market at all and whether the film is a last-ditch effort to make money. But good filmmakers, just like A-list actors, always look for a Unique Point of View (UPOV) in a script, so I wonder how the screenwriter, director, and actors deal with the phenomenon. Indeed, Robbie and co have managed to launch a new UPOV, making Barbie a story about patriarchy, feminism, the life of a modern woman, the roles of men and women. A story in which the Mattel brand isn't even glorified. It still puzzles me why so many women and men, after seeing the film, succumb to pink mania. I find the urge to stand in a Barbie packaging box for their very own Barbie moment completely incomprehensible.

La Terre vue du ciel – Earth from above

September 2000. I'm driving with a small crew consisting of a cameraman and a sound engineer to Le Grand-Hornu in Mons. I'm working as a reporter for a cultural programme on the Belgian national broadcast channel Canvas, and this job gives me the opportunity to ask questions to extraordinary people. I love my job.

> Le Grand-Hornu was once one of the largest coal mining sites in our country and is a beautiful example of neoclassical industrial heritage. After years of renovation, the site reopened as a museum for contemporary art and has since been renamed the Centre d'Innovation et de Design (the C.I.D.).

One of the first exhibitions is that of aerial photographer-ecologist Yann Arthus-Bertrand. And it is with him that I will have a conversation.

Arthus-Bertrand's life resembles that of an adventurer. Born into a family of jewellers, he began a career in filmmaking as a young man, only to open a zoo in the middle of France a bit later in life. Around his thirties, he spent three years living with the Maasai in Kenya to photograph a family of lions. For safety reasons, he often did this from a hot air balloon. From then on, he dedicated himself to this branch of photography: travelling around the world, he got into helicopters, airplanes, and hot air balloons to take pictures. This later resulted in the creation of the first photo agency specialised in aerial photography, Altitude. Once back, he became a journalist, reporter, and photographer specialising in major reports on themes of sport, wildlife, and aerial photography. He sold to *National Geographic*, photographed Dian Fossey with her gorillas, and covered ten Paris-Dakar rallies.

Under the patronage of UNESCO, he began to compile an inventory of the Earth at the beginning of this new millennium. This inventory is titled "La Terre vue du ciel" ("Earth from the air" or "Earth from above"). I meet the Frenchman at the time when he is travelling around the world with the photo exhibition. Arthus-Bertrand is incredibly charming, speaks calmly, and has something mysterious about him. He reminds me of Robert Redford in the movie *Out of Africa*.

As a photographer-witness, Yann Arthus-Bertrand aims to demonstrate that the pace and way natural resources are extracted, processed, and consumed are becoming unsustainable. He talks about how his aerial photographs reflect the changing natural landscapes and expressions of life, as well as the traces of humans and environmental degradation. It is intended to prompt the viewer to think about the evolution of the planet and the future of humanity.

When I look at his photos, I see how, through his unique perspective and composition, he reveals patterns, textures, and colours. He uses a combination of helicopters and hot air balloons to achieve the perfect camera angle for his images, which often focus on the relationship between humans and their environment. His images evoke emotion and provoke thought, making them both visually stunning and deeply meaningful.

The critiques on Yann's aerial photos range from beautiful to moralising and didactic. The exhibition comes at a time when people are not aware of climate change. Al Gore's film *The Inconvenient Truth* will not be released until six years later. But at that time, he is not disheartened by this. With each photo, he includes the geographical data so that other photographers can take a picture at the exact same location in a few years and compare the two results side by side. Time will tell.

I decided to include my encounter with Yann Arthus-Bertrand in this book because of his Unique Point of View. You can't get more literal than this. He combined a bird's-eye view with both aesthetics, ethics and long-term thinking. A Unique Point of View is never one thing but an unexpected combination. From what angle do you look at the world, and what do you decide to do with it?

Good to know: six years later, he was was made a Knight of the French Légion d›honneur (National Order of the Legion of Honour); in the US, they call him the French Al Gore. His book *La Terre vue du ciel* has since sold 7 million copies and been translated into 21 languages. The photos are also available for free download on his website.

Developing a UPOV doesn't happen overnight. And once you have one, you'll also work with the next three criteria to give more shape to your personality and give your UPOV more impact.

Conviction

If having substance is one criterion for developing personality in your personal branding, then a second is your 'conviction' or belief. Conviction refers to a deep faith and unwavering commitment to your values, principles, and the message you want to convey to your audience. It reflects the drive and sincerity you show in your actions, words, and overall brand identity.

In personality branding, conviction means being clear about your purpose, mission, and what you stand for. It means conveying your beliefs and ideas with genuine enthusiasm and showing the courage to remain true to your convictions, even when faced with challenges or criticism.

Let's now examine why it's as important as substance:

- **Strong emotional connection:** Substance forms the foundation of your personal brand, while conviction adds the emotional depth that helps you connect with your audience on a profound level. When your audience feels your genuine passion and conviction, they are more likely to resonate with your brand and develop a deeper, more meaningful connection with you.

- **Building trust and reliability:** Substance ensures your expertise and credibility, but conviction shows your commitment and sincerity. When your audience sees that you truly believe in what you do and stand for, it increases their trust in your brand and makes you more reliable in their eyes.

- **Differentiation and memorable branding:** While many people may possess the same knowledge and expertise, your conviction distinguishes you and makes your personality brand memorable. It's the passion and energy you bring to your brand that leaves a lasting impression on your audience.

- **Attracting like-minded individuals:** Conviction in your personality branding attracts like-minded individuals who share or want to share the same values and beliefs. These connections can lead to a strong community of ambassadors more inclined to commit to your brand and advocate for your message.

- **Resilience and consistency:** Having conviction in your personality helps you remain resilient and committed to your goals, even in tough times. It encourages consistency in your message and actions, which strengthens the authenticity of your brand.

So, while substance forms the foundation of credibility and knowledge in personality branding, conviction adds the emotional depth, passion, and sincerity that together build a strong connection with your audience. Having both is essential for creating a compelling and sustainable personality brand that resonates with others and leaves a lasting impact.

Working on your conviction involves tuning into those fundamental principles that guide your actions and shape your character. However, determining your values is not just a matter of picking words from a list that appeal to you. It requires introspection and a deeper investigation into what is truly important to you.

When determining your values, you might turn to Google to find a list of ideals that appeal to you. Here are the pitfalls when you engage in cherry-picking:

1. You choose what you're good at.
2. You select those of your company.
3. You choose values that you don't possess but would like to have.
4. You pick those that sound good and enhance your reputation.

But your real values go beyond superficial preferences. They are the values that evoke strong emotions in you – you feel lost, sad, or angry when they are not met. These core values are deeply embedded in your being and shape how you perceive the world.

Your most profound values can also be a double-edged sword. They can be so dear to you that you remain too faithful to them, and they force you into difficult choices. Feeling a healthy tension here, I believe, is a sign that you're on the right track. But definitely also be open to revising your values and how you apply them.

Remember that discovering and refining your conviction is an ongoing journey. As you delve into your values and how they align with your personal brand, be gentle with yourself. Embrace self-awareness and give yourself permission to grow and evolve.

In her book *Dare to Lead*, Brené Brown provides guidance for selecting your core values as a compass for leadership and decision-making. She emphasises the importance of identifying core values that align with one's personal and professional aspirations. She designed the selection process to ensure authenticity and congruence with one's actions and leadership style. They might help you in your quest:

- The first step is identifying a list of values that resonate with you. These can be principles or qualities you deeply believe in and want to embody in your leadership journey. Write down as many values as are meaningful to you.
- Then start narrowing down the initial list of values to a more manageable selection. Consider which values truly define who you are and align with your vision of leadership. Try to choose a handful of values that hold the most meaning for you.
- Make each value concrete: I find this the most important step. Look for examples in your life where you've made choices easily or with difficulty. Take the time to clarify and define each value you've selected. Reflect on what each value means to you personally and how it might manifest in your actions as a leader. This step helps you better understand the essence of each chosen value.
- Prioritise your values: After defining your values, you need to prioritise them based on their importance and relevance to your leadership approach. Consider which values are non-negotiable and fundamental to your character and leadership style.

- Align values with behaviour: It's crucial to align your chosen values with your actions and behaviour. Assess whether your daily decisions and interactions reflect the values you've identified. Aim to live and lead in accordance with your chosen principles.
- Communicate your values: As a leader, it's essential to communicate your values clearly and consistently with your team and stakeholders. Sharing your values fosters a sense of trust, transparency, and a shared purpose.
- Evaluate and adjust: Values are not static; they can evolve and change over time. Continuously review your values and adjust them as you grow and gain new experiences. Be open to refining or adding values that better fit your changing leadership journey.

By following these steps, Brené Brown encourages leaders to cultivate a strong foundation of values that guide their decision-making, actions, and interactions. It promotes a more authentic and impactful leadership style, which can contribute to building a compelling and influential personal brand as a leader.

Unfair advantage

After substance and conviction, you have a third criterion with which you can examine your personality and strengthen your personality brand: your unfair advantage.

I first came across the concept of unfair advantage with Carole Lamarque, CEO and founding partner of Duval Union Innovative Marketing and Talent CHĪTĀ, when I was working with her on her third book launch and accompanying keynote, *Zoonotic*. Her second book is titled *Unfair Advantage* and discusses how to apply the principle in businesses.

PODCAST ALERT
Listen to my conversation with **Carole**, and you'll discover how she tackles it.

Your unfair advantage is a unique and distinguishing quality, skill, or attribute that sets you apart from others in your field. It is something that gives you, as a business or expert, a competitive edge and enables you to excel or achieve success in a way that is difficult for others to imitate. Do not confuse it with a Unique Selling Proposition (USP). A USP is a marketing concept used in business to highlight a specific feature or benefit that makes a product or service different from competitors and more appealing to customers. It is focused on the product or service itself.

The difference, therefore, lies in their focus and scope: in personal branding, a USP may refer to a unique aspect, skill, or expertise you possess, making you stand out and distinguishing you from other professionals in your field. An unfair advantage goes beyond a single unique attribute and encompasses a combination of qualities, skills, experiences, or perspectives that are not easily copied by others. In personality branding, identifying and leveraging your unfair advantage means recognising the unique mix of experiences, talents, and perspectives that make you truly distinctive and authentic. It includes your life experiences, personality traits, unconventional skills, or a combination of factors that contribute to the individuality and impact of your personal brand. A combination that is difficult or impossible to imitate.

The more unexpected a combination is, the stronger it is. Think of the combination of an economist and stand-up comedian (like Flemish Kamal Kharmach) or scientist and stand-up comedian (Lieven Scheire, a CEO who also plays in a rock band...)

Let's look at the personality brand of a leadership coach who is also a motivational speaker. Her knowledge and expertise lie in leadership development and personal growth. She has a strong conviction to empower individuals to reach their full potential and lead fulfilling lives. Her USP could be her unique coaching methodology that delivers transformative results for clients.

Now, her unfair advantage could be that she is a former astronaut who has experience overcoming immense challenges and leading in high-pressure situations. This life experience distinguishes her from other motivational speakers and coaches and provides a unique perspective and credibility that others cannot match.

The three criteria discussed reinforce each other in building a strong, multidimensional personality brand: substance and conviction provide the foundation and emotional connection, while the unfair advantage adds a distinguishing benefit that makes your brand remarkable and difficult for others to imitate.

Style

There are four criteria from which you can shape and strengthen your personality, thereby developing a personality brand instead of just a personal brand. We have just discussed substance, conviction, and unfair advantage. The last criterion is style, and it is not the last by accident.

Style encompasses the way you speak, act, write, behave, perform, dress, and interact with others. The picture fits, but not in an obvious or straightforward way. On the contrary, it may even be slightly off-kilter. It is essentially the vehicle through which you communicate your substance, conviction, and unfair advantage to the outside world. It goes beyond just your appearance and includes the overall impression you leave on others through your actions and communication.

- **Speaking and writing style:** Your speaking and writing style reflect the tone, language, and communication approach you use to convey your ideas, messages, and expertise. It includes your choice of words, storytelling ability, and the clarity with which you express yourself.
- **Behavioural style:** Behavioural style refers to your mannerisms, body language, and overall behaviour in different situations. It involves how you conduct yourself, interact with others, and handle both successes and challenges.

- **Dress style:** Your style of dress relates to how you present yourself through clothing and personal grooming choices. It encompasses your sense of fashion, grooming habits, and the image you project through your appearance.
- **Performance style:** Performance style pertains to how you showcase your skills, expertise, or talent in your field. It involves the way you deliver speeches, conduct workshops, or engage with your audience.

Style plays a crucial role in personality branding because it shapes the way others perceive you and your brand. It strengthens your personality brand by:

- **Creating a lasting impression:** A clear and consistent style helps you stand out and be memorable to your audience. It enhances brand recall and recognition.
- **Building trust and reliability:** A congruent style that matches your content, conviction, and unfair advantage fosters trust and reliability among your audience. It shows that you are genuine and true to yourself.
- **Differentiating yourself:** Style sets you apart from others in your field. It adds a unique touch to your brand that others cannot easily replicate.

Again, congruence is crucial because it ensures that your style aligns with your content, conviction, and unfair advantage. If there is consistency between how you present yourself (style) and what you stand for (content), it strengthens your authenticity and credibility.

> Let's consider a personality brand of a renowned chef who is passionate about sustainable cooking and environmental activism. His conviction lies in promoting eco-friendly practices in the culinary world. His unfair advantage could be his experience as a marine biologist, giving him a unique perspective on sustainable seafood. To effectively highlight his personality brand, he adopts a down-to-earth and accessible speaking style, uses organic and eco-friendly materials in

his chef's attire, and incorporates plant-based ingredients in his dishes. His style of performance includes giving cooking demonstrations to the public that emphasise the importance of eco-friendly cooking. In this example, the chef's style is congruent with his content (sustainable cooking and activism), his conviction (passion for eco-friendly practices), and his unfair advantage (expertise in marine biology). In this regard, what you post on social media is an expression of your personal style, even if you use techniques and formats known and employed by millions of others.

You're only as good as your last haircut

While browsing through Netflix's offerings, I stop at a documentary by Martin Scorsese. Scorsese is a filmmaker par excellence with blockbusters like *The Wolf of Wall Street* (2013), *Gangs of New York* (2002), *Shutter Island* (2010), and *Taxi Driver* (1976) under his belt. I pause because he had made a documentary series about the life and personality of his remarkable friend Fran Lebowitz.

Lebowitz is an American author, speaker, and social commentator who has lived in New York for decades and, it seems, does not leave the city. Her circle of famous friends is impressive, one of her best friends being Andy Warhol. Fran's last book dates to 1994, but she continues to call herself a writer. One with writer's block. That writer's block, which has now lasted for 30 years, has been her best move because she decided to switch from writing to speaking. Something that turned out to suit her much better, because she could leverage more of her strengths.

She already had a sharp voice as a writer, but even more so as a speaker. She always says what's on her mind. She is a gifted storyteller with the ability to discuss complex themes in an entertaining and accessible way. Her live performances and interviews are often filled with hilarious anecdotes and unconventional thinking. Fran Lebowitz is known for the wide range of interests and topics she speaks and writes about. To give a few examples:

- She has a deep love of art, literature, film, and theatre. She often gives her unfiltered opinion on contemporary culture and the art world, and reports on cultural trends and shifts with witty commentary.
- As a proud resident of New York City, Fran Lebowitz offers a unique perspective on city life. She enjoys sharing her observations and anecdotes about living in the bustling metropolis and isn't afraid to critique the changes the city has undergone.
- She is a keen observer of human behaviour and interactions and likes to discuss the peculiarities and absurdities of human conduct, leading to humorous and sometimes ironic comments.
- Though not known as a political commentator, Fran Lebowitz has often expressed her views on social issues and political developments. Her insights and observations can be provocative and invite reflection.
- As a writer, she enjoys sharing her views on writing and literary works and occasionally has humorous comments on the challenges of writing.
- A sharp eye for social and cultural trends and phenomena. These too are scrutinised critically, offering a unique perspective on changes in society.

Can you see how fascinating a personality is that can speak on more than one theme? And how that feeds her substance?

> When you look at the criterion of conviction, Fran Lebowitz is known for her steadfast beliefs and candid approach to topics. She speaks openly and unreservedly, expressing her thoughts without conforming to prevailing opinions. Her determination to remain true to her own views has earned her a loyal and admiring following.
>
> In terms of unfair advantage, this provides a unique and distinct combination: a brilliant mind and sharp wit, original

> perspective, and the ability to present complex ideas in an accessible and entertaining manner, enabling her to captivate and provoke thought in her audience.

But Fran doesn't even need to open her mouth to immediately give the impression that she has created her own style category. For decades, she has worn the same garments, a uniform that she has honed to create a look as recognisable as that of the late Karl Lagerfeld. She has an unmistakable style that strengthens her personality brand. Her tailor-made suits, thick black glasses frames, and luxurious mane have become iconic and reflect her confidence and individuality. It makes her incredibly recognisable and reinforces her image as a respected and influential figure.

Did you know she always has her suits custom-made at Anderson & Sheppard, who also served Fred Astaire, Charlie Chaplin, and King Charles? Anderson & Sheppard only do men's suits, except that one time for Marlene Dietrich.

In terms of personal branding, Fran is the American equivalent of the Flemish writer Herman Brusselmans. I remember how nervous I was when I was about to interview him for my show on TV. I thought he would make fun of me with his celebrity sarcastic humour. But when I welcomed him and briefed him on the recording, it immediately became apparent how gentle and nervous he was, just like Fran.

I immediately gave in to a binge-watch of seven episodes. I was utterly fascinated by Fran's personality. Everything, absolutely everything I mentioned in this chapter, was not just present in her, but sharp and extreme. She had her own style in everything. And you either loved it or you didn't. If you want to learn how to cultivate congruent behaviour into a personality brand, watch *Pretend It's a City*. And brace yourself...

Be inspired by archetypes

It's not easy to map out these four criteria for yourself. Often, you are not even aware of them, but others can help you identify them. It's also possible the criteria are not balanced or pronounced enough, making you come across as too bland.

To find out what kind of personality you have or harbour within you, you could take a personality test. I'm not a fan of such tests, especially not of the labels they assign. They're meant to provide insight, which is good, but they often lead to passivity. How often do you hear someone say, "I am Blue", "I am XXX"? That's supposed to make it clear for everyone, and you're expected not only to understand what that means but also to know what to do with that information. If you decide to take a personality test, try different kinds of tests. There will be overlap, but you'll also find nuances. You'll get a better sense of the focus of each test and be able to place the results more accurately. Most importantly, remember you are not the result.

Let's assume that you do have insight into who you are, and can respond to the four criteria, but honestly, it could be sharper. Not so mainstream, not bland, ordinary. It's harsh to say, but ordinary is the nickname of most people, which becomes clear when you start on your personality branding. What you can then do is let yourself be inspired by archetypes. I hope you remember the verb I just used: inspire.

Carl Gustav Jung, the famous psychologist, described various archetypes as fundamental and universal characters that exist in humanity's collective unconscious. According to him, these archetypes play a significant role in shaping our behaviour, motivations, and personality. They are often used in developing personality tests, but also in writing and analysing scripts and novels, where you encounter versions or variations of these archetypes. Given that people and characters can possess multiple archetypal characteristics, I'll fire off some inspiration from film and literature. With which character do you identify, and why?

The Innocent: Dorothy from *The Wizard of Oz* embodies innocence. She is characterised by her quest for safety, her aim to return home, and her longing to make friends, despite her fear of the witch and her inexperience.

The Everyman (Woman): Frodo Baggins from *The Lord of the Rings*, who leads a simple life and is tasked with destroying the Ring, shows undaunted courage despite his physical limitations.

The Hero: Harry Potter, the hero of the eponymous series, is propelled by his goal to defeat Voldemort and fulfil his destiny, even though he often acts impulsively out of fear of failure.

The Caregiver: In *The Lord of the Rings*, Samwise Gamgee is loyal to his friend Frodo, despite his own insecurities.

The Explorer: Alice in Wonderland and Indiana Jones thirst for adventure, driven by their determination and knowledge, despite the dangers they face.

The Rebel: Katniss Everdeen from *The Hunger Games* fights for freedom and justice, driven by her determination to do what's right, despite her impulsiveness.

The Lover: Romeo, from Romeo and Juliet, is characterised by his deep commitment to Juliet and his quest for true love, despite his reckless behaviour.

The Jester: Deadpool, the Joker from the Marvel films, is notorious for his desire for entertainment and his ability to use humour as a shield, despite his tendency not to take things seriously.

The Sage: Yoda from *Star Wars*, the sage, is driven by his desire for knowledge and wisdom, while he fears the dark side.

The Magician: Gandalf, the magician from *The Lord of the Rings*, is characterised by his wish to protect Middle Earth and use power for good, despite his limitations as a mortal wizard.

The Ruler: King Arthur aims to create a just kingdom, despite the difficult decisions he must make.

If we take a stab at real people, we could recognise the following archetypes:
The Caregiver: Oprah Winfrey, media mogul and philanthropist, is known for her compassionate demeanour and dedication to helping others.
The Rebel: Lady Gaga, the pop singer and actress, is known for her quirky, provocative style and her continued willingness to break conventions.
The Creator: Bob Ross, the famed painter and television personality, could fit into the 'Creator' archetype. His calm, supportive demeanour and focus on creative expression have endeared him to millions.
The Explorer: Sir Richard Branson, the founder of Virgin Group, can be seen as an 'Explorer' archetype. He is known for his adventurous spirit and willingness to take risks in business.
The Sage: Stephen Hawking, the renowned physicist. Despite the limitations of his physical health, he tirelessly pursued knowledge and shared his insights with the world.

Have you noticed that with some examples, you could also link them to other archetypes? It's debatable whether the listed celebrities would agree with me, and perhaps they would prefer a different archetype to be associated with their name. After all, you are not an archetype. It is therefore essential to be aware of certain pitfalls when working with them. Here are some things you should NOT do:

1. Do not stereotype yourself: Avoid rigidly categorising yourself into one archetype or limiting your identity to archetypal descriptions. Archetypes are symbolic representations and should not constrain your understanding of your unique complexity as an individual.
2. Do not neglect self-reflection: Using archetypes to enhance your personality requires self-reflection and self-awareness. Do not skip this crucial process by assuming that merely knowing about archetypes will automatically strengthen your personality.
3. Do not over-identify with negative traits: While archetypes contain both positive and negative aspects, do not use them as an excuse to justify or amplify negative behaviour. Instead, focus on

transformation – cultivating the positive qualities associated with your archetypes.

4. Do not ignore your uniqueness: Everyone's personality is a mix of various influences, including upbringing, experiences, and individuality. Do not neglect your unique traits and qualities in favour of meeting archetypal ideals.
5. Do not use archetypes to compare or judge others: Everyone's journey is different, and we all have our own mix of archetypal qualities. Respect and appreciate the diversity of personality expressions in others.

See archetypes not as fixed labels but as a playful way to view yourself differently. Moreover, archetypes are flexible and can change over time as you develop and grow.

As a trained and experienced actor, 'working with archetypes' was not a separate course during my training. We didn't need it since we had to read and discuss 100 plays ranging from Vondel, Goethe, Shakespeare, to the present, per academic year. Do this, and you'll also understand what Jung was talking about.

Summary of Chapter 6: How is your personality doing?

A lot of things to remember:

1. Focus on congruency instead of authenticity. Congruency builds trust. Authenticity, not always.
2. Don't use authenticity as a cover-up. There is being authentic, being perceived as authentic, or presenting oneself as authentic.
3. Work on the four criteria of personality: Substance, Conviction, Unfair Advantage and Style.
4. Substance is not just the sum of your knowledge, expertise, experience, skills, but it adds your unique point of view on all of that as the cherry on the cake.
5. Conviction is not just a set of values; it is the courage you show to say no to great opportunities because they are not aligned with your values.
6. Unfair advantage can be that one thing that gives you an advantage that feels unfair to others. But it can also be a combination of things that no one else has.
7. Style is not only the way you dress, but also how you speak, write and behave. Make them different and congruent and you rock the personal branding process!
8. Look for role models or archetypes to get inspired but don't copy them.

PART 4: STORYTELLING

Chapter 7: Develop your narrative

A treasury of stories

I have taken you through the process I went through as an actor to create a character. I've talked about the journey of discovery while reading a script, alone or together with the crew. Reading dialogues, supplemented with actions, gives an idea but not necessarily a complete picture of a character and their personality. As an actor, you then search for possible background stories. The behaviour of a character or some personality traits do not come out of nowhere and are the result of past experiences. That experience isn't necessarily needed to tell the story, but it is to make choices in how you portray the personality. As an actor, you then conceive those stories that can bridge this gap yourself. In the later years of my acting career, screenwriters created what we called the 'bible', a document in which they included such stories. What was their childhood like, what education did they have, what life philosophies, what traumas had they suffered? It was a gold mine for an actor because it provided nourishment to their interpretation and the choices they had to make. These stories added depth and colour to dialogues and scenes.

But from the moment I started giving interviews, I soon realised that journalists were also looking for these kinds of stories. They wanted to know about my background, how I grew up, what my opinions were on various subjects. Predictably, they also sought to link the character I played to my own personality. If my character did X, they asked if I did that in my life or differently. I quickly became adept at giving interviews, seldom facing surprises because I always prepared for them. I decided in advance which stories I would share and in which situation. There were stories that kept reappearing, which I then could tell better and better each time. It was a balance between telling a story that was interesting enough, could not cause misleading headlines, and did not personally attack anyone. In doing so, I also began to search for what my voice exactly was. How did I feel most comfortable in being me: was it by making jokes, being distant, adopting a critical stance, or finding everything good and fun? When journalists interview you, they want to capture your personality in a document, a fragment, a montage. And in that, I wanted to have a say.

As an actor, you seek connection with your character by inventing stories around them. As a journalist, you aim to capture stories to connect your readership with the person you're interviewing. As an expert, and as a personal brand, you also need to connect with the target audience to whom you offer your products, services, knowledge, and personality, just as they need to connect with you so they can discover if you are worth their time and investment.

> ***"The most powerful person in the world is the storyteller"***
> — Steve Jobs

I want to help you discover the importance of storytelling and, more importantly, developing a narrative when shaping your personality brand. You'll learn about the stories you should always have ready-to-tell, like a handkerchief in your purse or your jacket. You never know when you might need them.

Learning to tell your story can help you in many ways. It can assist you in living in alignment with your personal values, purpose, and vision. It can also help attract people and connect you with others who share your values and vision.

However, because we always talk about "your story", it's too often assumed there can literally be only one, and that this story is unchangeable. But that's not true. You don't need just one story; you need a narrative.

What made you famous doesn't always keep you famous

I've always been cautious about lauding professionals who became famous for a single story. Relying on one story for your branding offers a deceptive impact. In my own professional life, I've encountered this and have always been careful with it.

Freshly graduated from the Royal Conservatory of Brussels as a Master of Arts (dramatic arts degree), having just turned 21, I acted in a theatre monologue, portrayed a role in a TV series about the work of writer Gerard Walschap, and played the now legendary Princess Prieeltje on our national broadcast VRT. I was lucky because I had a lot of work.

The role in *Ons Geluk* was ignored by the press, but portraying Princess Prieeltje in the TV series *Kulderzipken* captured the heart of the general public. While I myself stood on the film set with trembling knees alongside Belgian A-list actors like Jan Decleir, Warre Borgmans, Lucas Van den Eynde, and Michael Pas, my character was more confident, and bolder than I was at that point in my life.

The effect of this series on the audience was exceptional: viewers spoke the language that scriptwriter-philosopher Hugo Matthysen had invented, girls and mothers asked for the dress I wore and wanted to replicate it, fathers and sons fell in love with Prieeltje and couldn't hide it when I entered the room, and babies were named after me or my character.

Twenty episodes were recorded between 1993 and 1995. And the series is still being rebroadcast annually, some 30 years later. Men and boys still blush, and girls still dream. This is the beautiful side of the coin. There's another side, though.

I became the New Talent On The Block but at the same time I was stigmatised in the following years by directors, production houses, and broadcasters. The role had branded me too strongly. At that time, it was believed that the television-viewing public wouldn't accept me in a different role. I didn't just play Prieeltje... I became her. The same was true in theatre, where it was often assumed that your credibility as a theatre actor diminished if you were also a television actor. What made me known also burned me. And I had to look for a strategy to help me out of this.

> An example of a very different calibre is J.K. Rowling. She became world famous overnight with the publication of her book *Harry Potter and the Philosopher's Stone* (1997). Nobody had heard of her till then – besides the publishers that had rejected her manuscript. Seven books, movies, and millions in her bank account later, she faced a problem. Her success had hijacked the continuation of her writing career. Rowling now writes under pseudonyms.

As an artist, painter, or writer, you soon encounter this dilemma in your work. You are, after all, a creative being, a being that wants to push boundaries, explore, and work and think out of the box. You don't want to play the same type of roles for ten years, paint the same type of work.

It was also a startling realisation for me that this was the case in the business world. Time and again, I was pointed to the idea of thinking in a niche, having one focus, standing for one thing so that everyone knows you for that one thing. That thing was then the product or service you sold, or the company you worked for. The goal was to generate revenue, and fame helped with that. But if you wanted to grow into another 'thing', did you then lose your credibility and have to start all over again?

Because, okay, focusing on what you do business-wise makes sense. But I don't think applying the same strategy to your personal branding is the right approach. Company branding, product branding, employer branding, and personal branding have overlaps but don't overlap 100%.

In my contacts and work with experts, entrepreneurs, and C-suite, I notice daily that this doesn't work. CEOs come to me and tell me – almost whispering – that they want to take a different personal direction. That they have outgrown their company and want to move on. That they have so much more and different things to offer, but there's no room for it. They don't know how to move on to the next phase in their career or how to start a new company without losing their credibility.

Immersing yourself in one kind of expertise and becoming the best at it is the strategy that will yield the most business-wise. But if you want to grow, you need a different strategy. One in which personal branding plays a strategic role, and creating a body of work and an accompanying narrative is the path to it.

A narrative is not just any story

It's confusing: storytelling, own your story, and now a narrative. So let's quickly clarify the differences:

A story is a narration consisting of a beginning, middle, and end (Aristotle) and features a tension arc where a character is pulled from their normal life, must overcome an obstacle, faces an enemy, then works towards a solution (good or bad) and becomes a hero (Gustav Freytag). It's also called the hero's journey (Joseph Campbell).

Storytelling is a strategy to persuade people of something and thereby move them to action. In a business context, this will almost always lead to a sale.

A narrative, on the other hand, is more than just a story. It's how various stories are interpreted, organised, and presented. A narrative can also contain opinions, context, values, and interpretations. It's about the perspective and meaning given to events and can change the sequence of events to emphasise a particular point or elicit a certain reaction from the audience.

So, essentially, while a story is what literally happens, a narrative is how and why the story is told. In terms of personality branding, your story may include the facts of your life and career, while your narrative is the unique spin you put on those facts to shape and communicate your personal brand. It also tells something about your values and your purpose.

So, in fact, my book should actually be called Own Your Narrative because that's what I mean. But because my readers, including you, feel and know the word 'story' much better, I use that.

So, in your narrative, you can have different stories and storylines which is good news because then you have more freedom to vary, to evolve, and not to become a bore to your audience.

Here are some questions that can help you find the stories in your life:

- What is the hardest thing you've ever done? What did you learn about yourself from that challenge? How have you used those lessons to make tough decisions?
- Who are the two people who have had the biggest impact on your life? What did you learn from them? Which events in your life show how you've applied the lessons learned from those mentors?
- What was your first job, and what valuable lessons did you learn there? Describe incidents that reveal some of the challenges and insights you gained from doing that work.
- What is your proudest memory? Why? Write down that story in as much detail as possible.
- How would you like to be remembered? Which event in your life so far best illustrates that you are the person you want to be remembered as? Write down that story.

- If you're like me, you have a plethora of stories, not all of which are professionally deployable. Choose what you can use in your professional life and reflect on the reason.
- These prompts not only help in discovering stories that define you but also in understanding how these narratives can be woven into your personal or professional branding, enriching the way you present yourself to the world.

A narrative has two buckets of stories. The first one contains the Core4; the other one, the CC4.

The Core4 are four kinds of stories where you are the protagonist; your audience is in the CC4. Let's first dive into the Core4.

Bucket 1: Your Core4

Developing your background story

People are always curious about your background story, your 'origin story'. And no, we don't want to hear a story that starts at your birth and goes through all the years of your life with dates and names. We want to find out which experiences have made you into the person and professional you are today.

In crafting your background story, you work on creating a narrative about what in your past has led you to become who you are now, do what you do now, and think what you think now. In this story, you can talk about your private life, or moments in your professional career, or both. Your background story is not just a list of events, nor is it just an anecdote. It consists of multiple layers: the base is who you are and how you developed in your early life – your character traits. The second layer reflects your goals and values – what you believe in and strive for as you grow older. The final layer is your stories – what you choose to remember about your past and how you make it meaningful now and in the future.

You can have multiple background stories to pick from. So, think about which story to tell on what occasion.

When developing your narrative, you make use of your portfolio and your oeuvre. By reading this book, you have already read various facets of my origin story. Each time, they aimed to provide a certain lesson learned while simultaneously giving you insight into my past. This also gives you an idea of how my expertise was developed, which has made me who I am today. But I choose which storylines or stories I tell when.

Your 'Fail Forward' storyline

> *"Bad choices make good stories"*
> (a quote I once saw printed on a jacket)

You are not perfect and there is no need to pretend you are. Everyone has failed at least once in his or her (professional) life. You have too. But have you ever dared to talk about it?

After the bankruptcy of her company, Flemish entrepreneur Sylvia Feytons wanted to break the taboo surrounding failure and open it to discussion. In Flanders in 2017, failing was hard, and talking about it, even harder. Together with Karen Boers and with the support of the Flemish government, she launched Failing Forward (or in Dutch 'met falen en opstaan'), a broad (government) campaign aimed at creating awareness about entrepreneurial failure and breaking the taboo on failing and making mistakes. The ultimate goal of this four-year campaign was to initiate a cultural change. I was one of the first batch of ambassadors, along with economist Geert Noels, technology futurist Peter Hinssen, the late athlete Marieke Vervoort, and others, who helped make failing in business a topic for discussion by sharing their own failure story. And although I was used to sometimes failing at rehearsals by playing a scene terribly badly as an actor, it was a victory for me to talk about the failure of my crowdfunded novel in front of an audience.

Internationally, there are the Fuckup Nights, a global movement with a platform for international events where people can share their personal failure stories. Every month, various events take place worldwide where three to four speakers stand in the spotlight in front of a room full of strangers to share their screw-ups. They talk about their companies going bankrupt, partnership agreements that fail, or products that must be recalled.

Telling a story about how you failed at a moment in your life and learned lessons from it makes you appear more human and, strangely enough, stronger. Moreover, it can help others deal with the mistakes they make or help prevent them.

When my son was still a child and a big fan of gaming YouTubers, I visited a fair with him to hunt for an autograph from his idol. We were queuing in a long line full of noisy teenagers. In front of me stood a girl with the following text printed on the back of her jacket: "Bad choices make good stories."

That text was absolutely right. A failure story contains all the elements of storytelling: a character, a setting, an event that disrupts everything, obstacles, and an ending. In this case, a bad ending because it's a failure story. Or is it? Indeed, a sad or bad ending doesn't have to be the definitive ending but can equally be the beginning of a new story.

The story of Sylvia's bankruptcy of her dream company, Book in a Box, had a sad ending from which she suffered greatly. However, she found the courage to draw lessons from it and use it as a fertile ground for new plans. This failure story was then utilised when she launched the Failing Forward campaign, which had a good ending.

Fortunately, Sylvia took the time to grieve first. And that is very important when you decide to come out with a failure story. Compare it with the pain you feel when you have an open wound versus a scar. A scar can still feel sensitive and painful both physically and mentally. But that's nothing compared to an open wound. Therefore, make sure that by the time you work on your failure story, it has become a scar.

A common difficulty in developing your failure story is finding the right words. I worked with an entrepreneur on a talk about her new startup. However, the story was overshadowed by a painful experience due to collaboration with people she loved. It caused her voice to tremble every time. As an actor, this is a recognisable moment in almost every creative process: not only your character but also you yourself have to be exposed. Being surrounded by supportive people who help you overcome the obstacle, even if it happens through tears, is then important. Once you've made it through, it gets easier every time. That's what I did with the entrepreneur. We went through her sorrow as she delivered her keynote aloud during our sessions. We searched for words that made her voice tremble less and sentences that offered more protection and support. Through the exercise, she worked on her resilience and strength. After our sessions, she could present her background and failure story powerfully.

> And what about Braden Wallake? You might not recognise this name but perhaps you will recognise his nickname, which he now wears like a crown on his LinkedIn header: The Crying CEO. His most viewed post on LinkedIn is from August 9, 2022, where he posted a video of himself crying. It received 58,000 likes, 10,539 comments, and 1,097 reposts because he publicly admitted his personal failure as a CEO. A few months earlier, he had made a bad decision and stayed too stubborn about it for too long. The result was that he had to lay off some employees. He found it unforgivable because his company is a 'people first' company, and he had just breached that trust. He published a crying CEO selfie with his text on LinkedIn, a professional platform. It made him an easy target. Opinions could not be more divergent and extreme, ranging from "CEOs can also cry" to "What a narcissist".

Who knows what the real story is? His text is indeed more sincere and stronger as a failure story than the photo. The message gets lost due to the interpretive possibilities of the image. For me, it's primarily the profile headline that tells the real story. After all, if you are still flaunting going viral from what should have been an authentically vulnerable moment a year later, and you wear your nickname like a crown, then something else is going on. You are no longer credible.

Your success story with challenges

Incorporating elements of failure into your background story is always an option, just as incorporating elements of success is. After all, these experiences have shaped you into who you are today. So why tell a separate failure story? Because it allows you to focus purely on one particular lesson learned or impact. Because this story can be used at different times and for different reasons in your communication.

The same applies to a success story. For many people, talking about their success is just as difficult as talking about their failures. It can come across as vain. However, this is not only person-specific but also culture-specific. The American entrepreneurs I have met have much fewer reservations. Also, they do not understand why we are not prouder of our successes.

Not so long ago, I caught myself unable to articulate what had made me successful. I was unprepared for the fact that an entrepreneur wanted to hear how I had managed to transform so successfully in my career. I had already processed other success experiences into a story, but I had not yet considered how I can easily move from one career change to another. I stumbled through my process and realised that I had not yet given it enough thought, let alone made it into an engaging story that someone else could learn from.

You have far more stories within you than you realise, and each story can have a place in your narrative where it serves a purpose for you and others. In this sense, your narrative complements your oeuvre perfectly; it is your narrative oeuvre. It was, in fact, through that conversation that I began to think about it. Meanwhile, I have also found part of the answer, and it is incorporated into this book. I started working with the concept of an oeuvre very early on. Creating a portfolio instead of a CV and developing a narrative soon became part of my path.

Your North Star story

The fourth Core4 story in your narrative that you can always carry with you and that will give your personality character is the story of your North Star. To grasp the profound significance of this story, I want you to visualise the moment you literally need the North Star. The North Star is the star that stands almost directly in the earth's northern celestial pole. It's the only bright star in the sky that doesn't move. It's a more consistent navigation tool than a magnetic compass. In other words: if you're lost, you can always find your way back with the help of the North Star.

Do you also have a North Star? A reference point to which you can connect everything you do and dream. That guides you in making choices on the way there. That shows you the way in making decisions and taking actions? Can you tell us about it in a way that makes us feel and understand how important it is to you?

Bucket 2: Your CC4

The Core4 is your first bucket of stories in your narrative. In the Core4 stories you are the protagonist. The second bucket contains the CC4 stories, or the Customer-Centric Stories. Stories where your customer is the protagonist.

I often see professionals only tell stories about their clients, about how they want to serve them, even on the 'about us' page of their website. I not only find that annoying but most of all disrespectful. If a company or expert doesn't give me – a potential client – the opportunity to find out more about the people in the company, how am I supposed to trust?

Customer-Centric Stories are an important part of your narrative, but in the personality branding process, it cannot overrule the Core4. Customers buy from YOU, as a personality brand. They choose because of YOU.

Let's dive in to the four main Customer-Centric Stories.

- **The I-know-how-you-feel story:** You are on their side and identify with their emotions. Stories in which you talk about yourself or others who have a similar problem and how it was or was not resolved.

- **The vision story:** You inspire people and encourage them to feel hope or happiness. This is where you convince your audience that their hard work and sacrifice is worth it. Use vision stories when you need to motivate people to change their behaviour. They can inspire people to overcome the frustrations, obstacles and challenges that come with change. And maybe you have a product or service that helps them with this.

- **The values-in-action stories:** Stories where you reinforce the values/mindset you want your audience to demonstrate or think about.

- **Customer success stories:** Probably the best known and used stories because these are the use cases, case studies or long-form testimonials where clients talk about their journey in working with you.

Applying your narrative

The Core4 stories belong in your narrative as a personality brand because they amplify your personality. Your CC4 stories connect you with your audience so they know you know them. These two buckets of stories build a meaningful narrative when you incorporate your values and lessons learned into each story, rather than just telling an anecdote. Remember, you can let them live, change them, adapt them, and seek new ones. Each bucket can have multiple stories to tell.

Stories from your narrative can be utilised in various ways in your communication: on your website, incorporated as a post or video, in interviews, during meetings, you name it.

By offering a narrative, I aim to provide an alternative to brand stories that can feel carved in stone. You are a person, and therefore by definition a moving, living being with evolving thought.

Summary of Chapter 7: Develop your narrative

7 things to remember:

1. Personal branding thrives on storytelling.
2. Storytelling is a strategy to persuade, emotionally connect and get people into action.
3. A narrative is a collection of stories you use with a goal in mind.
4. A narrative is not static; it can change over time.
5. A narrative has two buckets of stories. The first one contains the Core4, the other one the CC4.
6. The Core4 are four kinds of stories where you are the protagonist, like your background story, Fail Forward story, success story, and North Star story.
7. In the CC4, your audience is the protagonist: the I-know-how-you-feel story, the vision story, the values-in-action stories and customer success stories.

Chapter 8: Who are you telling your stories to?

The great absentee

Have you ever realised that there's always one family member missing from the vacation photos you took as a child with your family or with your own children? And often, you only realise this years later? The great absentee in your family album is the person who captured your memories. In some families, it's often the same person who takes the photos because it was a hobby, or they were the only one who had a talent for it.

In this book, the great absentee so far has been your audience or your target group. And perhaps you've even been annoyed by the fact that I haven't emphasised its importance from page one. Because that's what you read about everywhere – in social media, content writing, marketing, and all types of branding articles.

So why do I, someone with a background in entertaining an audience, bring this up in the middle of the book? Well, precisely for that reason. I want to prevent you from basing your identity, your personality on what your audience wants to see from you or your ideal customer needs from you. My wish and goal for you is that you first have a clear vision of how your personality comes across best. What you want to stand for, how you want to be seen, what your North Star is. I want you to be imbued with that, to know and feel your stories.

Only then do you look at who is in your audience, who your target group is. Do you have an audience to whom you want to sell? Does your audience resonate with who you are? If yes, great. If not, what will you do? Adjust your audience? Adjust your personal brand? Have someone else be the face of your company?

These are three possible options, of which option two is the hardest because you will then work with a stage persona that may not be for the long term and also may not feel authentic. But it's possible. The third option is also realistic if your ego allows it. After all, you're not always the best person to represent a company on social media. It's important to realise that and find your place. It may also be that your target group has segments, and you're a perfect fit for one but not for another. How will you know that if you don't know what you want first?

Mind the gap

"Mind the gap" is a warning you not only need to heed in the London Underground but also here. There's the gap between who you are and who you want to be as a person, the gap you're supposed to bridge as a business leader, the gap in how you're supposed to act as an employer. Mapping out how big or small this gap is, and how you can bridge it without having to do the splits, is the work that needs to be done. Because one way or another, you're not standing with both feet on one side but with one on each side.

In a world where customer-centricity and employee engagement have become so important, I find people pleasing to be the most dangerous consequence of all strategies, visions, and methodologies. Those who engage in too much people pleasing in company branding, employer branding, and personal branding also create a 'too much' feeling among the same audience. Over time, customers, employees, and followers also notice that you're not authentic enough, that you're too much of a follower rather than a company, an employer, a person with character.

Do you think Picasso had an ideal customer in mind before starting new work? When artists are not working on commission, they do as they please. Even when they are working on commission, it might still be the case. You choose them for who they are and what they do.

Once the match is found between your personality and an audience that embraces that and wants to buy from you, you can much more easily proceed with your communication, your content creation. You don't have to bend over backward, be more accessible or more pretentious than you can handle, you don't have to use a different language.

Wouldn't that be wonderful?

And yet, in reality, it won't be that easy. I'll share an experience that 'initiated' me as an actor in learning how to deal with very different audiences who each had a right to their opinion, feedback, behaviour, and criticism of how I performed.

Of all those who have nothing to say, those who remain silent are the most pleasant.

The first theatre role I landed as a freshly graduated 21-year-old actor from the Royal Conservatory in Brussels was that of a teenage girl in a monologue. For an hour and a half, I stood alone on stage, speaking to a usually full room, sometimes less packed, of people who had paid for their ticket, dressed up, booked a babysitter, and braved the weather, winds, and traffic to see me, because I had a story to tell that – according to the brochure – was worth their time and through which they hoped to have a beautiful, unforgettable evening. For 90 minutes, I gave my best to ensure that the title of the play would NOT be proven true:

> ***"Of all those who have nothing to say, those who remain silent are the most pleasant."***

Of all those who have nothing to say, those who remain silent are the most pleasant

This title was a godsend for theatre critics who didn't like it. A title like that was simply asking for trouble in the press.

It's 1994, and back then, we had brutally harsh theatre critics in Flanders who were feared by everyone. They could make or break an actor's career and performance, and the ticket sales. I was easy prey if I did not perform.

But as if that wasn't enough, the writer-director of the play, Frank Theys, had written a monologue about a teenage girl who, musing in her bedroom, leans over her desk and brings forth teenage wisdom. The girl was half in thought, hanging, mumbling incoherently. Half sentences, sounds, sighs, clichés, ... was all you got to hear.

There was no dramatic arc, no grand storytelling, no action. Or, well... There was action, but of a completely different kind. My character was constantly sucking on a pen. And those among you who have done this know that, eventually, you'll bite through it and get ink on your fingers and mouth. Well, that's what happened to my character too. After a while, my mouth was also full of ink. That was the moment I looked forward to. I was curious about who in the audience would give me – the actor – signals to save me from embarrassment. Who in the audience would start to giggle, who would feel ashamed and start to fidget in their seat? From the corner of my eye, I followed the audience; they thought I couldn't see them. For them, I was lost in thought.

But nothing could be further from the truth.

My pen was actually prepared to release ink. Before each performance, I filled the sponge we had attached to it with ink, and initially I had to make sure it didn't start dripping too early. And in every performance, I enjoyed how a musing teenage girl could wrap a room full of people around her finger with half sentences.

The monologue was a game of attraction and repulsion. Looking and daydreaming. You're allowed into my world and sometimes I see you and sometimes I ignore you. My character allowed you to observe her and peek into her personal little life. And sometimes she slammed the door shut. Like teenagers do.

For eight weeks, the director and I locked ourselves in the black box of a rehearsal space filled with decrepit stuff you were allowed to 'play' with. For hours on end, for this one man, I practised the strange incoherent words out loud and looked for how I could give them meaning, the feeling that my character wanted to go somewhere but didn't yet know where. How I could make her real and authentic? As an actress, I wanted to know what she was looking for, otherwise I would just be floundering. The director saw me as a piece of videotape that he could endlessly replay and edit. I couldn't blame him; he was actually a filmmaker and not a theatre director. But he exhausted me and made me do everything over and over again. After a six-hour rehearsal day of talking, I was exhausted and my throat hurt. The drilling strengthened my muscles, my resilience, it made my voice grow despite the fatigue. Fortunately, I had danced all my life and was used to pushing through despite pain and fatigue.

The fear I had of critics proved to be unfounded. The reviews were great, and the performances often sold out. Five nights a week, I drove through Flanders and the Netherlands in my first second-hand self-financed little car, discovering how many cultural centres, theatre halls, and parish halls there were. In the evening rush hour – when people were heading home – I drove to my 'work', which was entertaining people who had worked all day. I discovered that the audience on one side of the country reacted differently than that on the other side, that a quiet audience was not necessarily an uninterested audience. That Dutch people found the Flemish language incredibly cute (there is a difference in accent, it's like UK English versus US English). That some jokes landed quicker in some places than in others. That one theatre hall could be a nightmare in terms of acoustics and another a dream.

But I also learned that the performance didn't work at all for the age peers of the character I played. Performing for secondary school kids was a whole different ballgame than the evening performances. If I performed as I did during the evening shows and as the director wanted, the teenagers in the audience felt downright offended. I held up a mirror to them and became 'the enemy'. And they made that very clear.

To earn their interest and attention, I had to make them accomplices in my character's quest. They had to become MY gang members.

So, I started making small adjustments. I gave different looks, changed intonations, looked at them personally... Those who talked back the most became my accomplices. In the dark, they always felt strong, but when I gave them my light, it looked different. It was a matter of weighing and balancing, trying out a lot and working hard to make 300 teenagers from different schools listen to you, that red-haired girl on a stage, for an hour and a half.

If the director came to one of those school performances, I would get scolded in the dressing room afterwards because I hadn't played the character according to his vision. I was glad I had survived.

When people come to me and say they are afraid of their (adult) audience, it's time they understood what it's like to stand in front of a room of exploding hormones. (Self)relativisation is an important part of the job.

Five nights a week, travelling hundreds of kilometres to a place you don't know – back then without GPS, mobile phone, or even wifi – while you're still naive and green. Arriving in an unfamiliar city and finding your way to the theatre. Being welcomed by strangers who show you the way to the hall. There, the only familiar face you come across, to whom you entrust everything: your theatre technician. Usually men, sometimes women, who have been working all day for this performance. Who lug your decor and the spotlights. Who build for hours before the curtain opens. Who ensure you have light and sound during the performance every night and who break everything down again for the next hall in the next city in another country. When I felt too lonely on stage, I looked into the dark, all the way to the back. That small light point... it was there.

For two years and more than 100 performances, I played the monologue. It got me a nomination for best actress at a Dutch theatre festival. Alain Platel, an internationally renowned director and one of the most influential choreographers in Belgium, with whom I had once worked, told me not so long ago that I had introduced an acting style in the theatre landscape that was innovative. Whatever it was, after that monologue, I felt I could take on the world. I had been initiated.

A three-dimensional story that converts

What I had done out of necessity, intuitively, from 'the gut' as artists call it, was to make a story for one target group also a story for another target group. A story that also converts for them. Actually, I had 'sold' the story to the teenagers.

And for that, I had the same words at my disposal, the same instrument (myself). All I did was tune interpretation, intonation, interaction, meaning, signals, body language to the world of a room full of teenagers.

What I did was make a story about my character into a story that was recognisable for an audience, and for which the time was ripe to tell this story. I made the story three-dimensional: a story of ME, a story of US, and a story of NOW.

But depending on the audience, I had to make adjustments. Because parents and teenagers look at each other through contradictory lenses. For the parents, I created the recognition of their struggling teenage child where one moment you are doubling over with laughter and the next you are tearing your hair out. For the teenagers, I had to create a teenage view of another teenager if they were to go along with my story. A look that said 'I understand you'.

The 3D technique is one of the most important techniques in storytelling, one that is used in good TED Talks. Use this well and you can take your place in the category of 'inspiring and motivating' speaker. The only downside is that it can become terribly cheesy. So once again: use it in moderation.

Summary of Chapter 8: Who are you telling your stories to?

5 things to remember:

1. Just because we haven't talked about them doesn't mean they aren't important: your audience.
2. Make sure you have a good fit between you, your personal brand and your audience or you won't last.
3. The same story will come across differently to different audiences.
4. Make a story three-dimensional so your story is recognisable to your audience and relevant to the moment you tell it.
5. Three-dimensional stories convert best.

PART 5: THE PROCESS

In Part 2 of this book, you read about why I recommend engaging in personal branding. I provided reasons for why it's a good marketing strategy, driven by investors, customers, and employees. But also that legacy building is another reason that is just as important. I introduced you to the concept of oeuvre thinking. With Part 3, I hope to have conveyed the importance of personality. What you've read and experienced should now be considered as the marinade in which you'll soak the next part.

In this final part, things become very concrete. Personal branding is about content creation, and there's no escaping it. What content and in what form can be discussed. It's time to step out and get to work.

> ***If a tree falls in the forest, and nobody is around to hear it, does it make a sound?***

"Mind-blowing." That's what I thought when I read the book *Sapiens* by Israeli historian and philosopher Yuval Noah Harari. Even more so, he articulated something I had always thought: that religions and societies are narratives we've created to establish connections and agreements among people in an overly large group.

I had often brought this up in discussions with friends. Unfortunately, I was met with strange, uncomprehending looks and my voice was either ignored or silenced. Of course, I am not Harari, and at that time, his book hadn't even been published. Now, when I bring it up, I attribute that same thought to Harari, for the simple reason that his voice is the loudest and most heard. It even seems silly to claim that I had always thought the same. Where would I get such insights?

Exactly. "Where would 'someone like me' get such insights?" That's the question people ask themselves when you claim something out of the ordinary. You too, as you just read this. A rapid analysis is made in our brains. You are scanned based on what is known about your past, your education, your personality, your appearance, your lifestyle, your social media posts, your work, and your interactions and relationships with people. Whether the sources drawn upon are legitimate or not, it gets mixed into a soup that needs to be blended. Three seconds later, a judgement is ready:

Yes, I believe you.
No, I don't believe you.
Wait, what are you saying?

We always believe we are right.

If there's one thing in abundance, it's opinions. Descartes would turn in his grave if we were to start saying now: "I have an opinion, therefore I exist." In his *Discours de la méthode* (1637), the French philosopher and mathematician wrote 'Je pense, donc je suis' (I think, therefore I am). It was his response to the quest for certainty. After all, our senses can deceive. Now, if you assume that you had better doubt everything, then you can be sure of one thing: there is someone who doubts. And doubting, says Descartes, is tantamount to thinking.

And now, you and I are inundated with opinions that seem to have the sole purpose of convincing us of their Absolute Rightness. And we do the same. You express your opinion because you want to show that you exist and do not doubt. The Flemish philosopher Ruben Mersch wrote no less than two books about having, sharing, and dealing with differing opinions. I can certainly recommend them.

"Our brain tortures reality until it confesses what we want to hear," writes Mersch in his book *Van mening verschillen* (Differing Opinions). You only look for evidence that what you think is true. I too searched for the above quote because it aligns with my view. It was convenient that Harari thought the same as me. He may have taken the credit, but I can live with that. I use him as a glamorous quote in this book and in keynotes :)

A contemporary of Descartes, George Berkeley, came up with the following thought experiment: "If a tree falls in a forest and no one is around to hear it, does it make a sound?"

From a scientific standpoint, the answer is that there will be vibrations. But these vibrations can only be called sound if they are captured and recognised as sound in our nerve centres. In other words: if there is no one to perceive the tree, there is no sound. It sounded logical. In the 17th century.

But what if a camera with a microphone filmed the falling tree and later this video is shown on social media and television among all other videos of falling trees. Is there then an absolute certainty that the tree from our video is heard?

Let's take it a step further. What if 30 trees were to fall in the forest at the same time. And this time, you are there. Would you have heard the fall of that one tree? Or would you look at the one that remained standing?

Back to my initial story. Suppose Harari had not introduced that idea into the world, and the path was clear for you and me. What would we need to do to have an equal impact?

What steps would you need to take to make your insight known to an audience that extends beyond your customer base, the audience of your network organisation, or your social media following? So, how do you ensure that your tree stands out among all the others?

Chapter 9: Overnight success

You've never heard of them before, and suddenly, they are everywhere. Every year, there's someone who captures the media's attention and becomes inescapable on social media. They achieve success overnight because they did something that grabbed attention. However, what no one can predict at that moment is whether you're a flash in the pan or the upcoming star.

The one-hit wonder

The one-hit wonder is most commonly associated with the music industry. Take global hits like "Macarena" (1996) and La Roux's "Bulletproof" (2009), for instance. The artists made a fortune off their hit, but that's where it ended. However, on platforms like LinkedIn, people can go viral with a post without it leading to significant, especially positive, changes in their careers.

In 2020, the year when Covid-19 hit and drove everyone from their offices to their living rooms to meet via Zoom, American HR consultant Lauren Griffiths changed her LinkedIn profile picture. You might think it was a minor, insignificant action that wouldn't even have been noticed had she not written a post about it. Here's what it said:

> "Why I Changed my LinkedIn Profile Pic
>
> Recently, I took a long hard look at my LinkedIn profile photo – the woman staring back at me had newly highlighted hair and a fresh cut, a pressed blazer, a hint of a smile that

showed just the right amount of teeth to let you know she was serious but could be lighthearted when needed. I remember standing in my power pose as my husband snapped the photos. We poured [sic] through about 80 shots before we found the one that looked perfectly polished. But the person I was exuding then is not always who I am, and certainly, not who I am right now.

Today's remote world has blurred the lines between my professional and personal selves, so I've chosen to represent that in my photo. Barely dried hair, comfy pullover, ripped jeans – slightly frazzled from having just gotten 3 kids ready for "school" – but smiling and ready for work.

I've witnessed and read enough on authentic leadership to know that being genuine and vulnerable will get you a lot farther in your career than a glossy headshot."

This post garnered her 876,887 views, 29,863 reactions, and 11,769 reposts. Why did it go viral?

If she had posted that same photo three years earlier, it would have been considered inappropriate on a professional platform like LinkedIn, especially for someone working for a corporate company. But then a pandemic rendered all such norms absurd.

Lauren was tired of fitting into a mould at a time when the world and her own family required something completely different. Her message resonated, triggering a wave of emotions and responses. Lauren challenged the status quo at just the right moment. The reach of this single post was phenomenal; her follower count surged to 20K. She was invited for interviews for a while, but that's where it ended. Lauren's website has gone offline, and since that one post, she has scarcely contributed her own content on LinkedIn.

Of course, there are also unexpected successes that have facilitated the breakthrough of a career. Since you, as a reader of this book, are likely not pursuing an artistic career, I will give you examples of the three media that can cause 'overnight success' in the business world and that also facilitate the transition to the status of personal brand and thought leader:

1. Write an international bestseller business book (author).
2. Deliver a TED Talk (keynote speaker).
3. Go viral on social media (social media influencer).

Feeling the pressure yet?

Write an international bestseller

> In 2011, Yuval Noah Harari, a young historian at the Hebrew University of Jerusalem, published a book based on a series of world history lectures he had taught. Harari, who had previously written about aspects of medieval and early modern warfare, but whose intellectual appetite from a young age was for comprehensive accounts of the world, wrote in sentences that did not succumb to the difficult-to-read academic language. The book, published in Hebrew as *A Brief History of Humankind*, became an Israeli bestseller. In 2015, the book was translated into English under the title *Sapiens*. It made *The New York Times* bestseller list and remained there for 182 weeks, including 96 consecutive weeks. Since then, it has been translated into 65 languages.

Sapiens catapulted him into a highly sought-after opinion leader who is not universally liked. Some call him controversial and a populist. Since then, Harari has travelled the world sharing his opinions and vision on a wide range of topics.

He could have stopped at various points had he not wanted this success. It is somewhat unusual for a historian, an academic, to live so visibly. He could have chosen not to have his book translated into English. Or to not change the title. He could have stopped after writing just one book, or refused to give lectures and interviews around the world. He certainly wouldn't have been the first or only one to refuse. But he wanted it and was also capable of doing it.

Since *Sapiens*, he has written more books and released various editions of *Sapiens*. Additionally, he maintains a strict routine and disciplined lifestyle in which two hours of daily meditation is a staple.

Deliver a TED Talk

In 2010, Brené Brown delivered a TED Talk. The American research professor, who studied shame, vulnerability, and leadership, spoke at TEDxHouston on the topic for the first time without shying away from her personal experience with the subject matter. She talked about her somewhat neurotic urge to measure unquantifiable things like emotions to gain control over them. When she was introduced as a 'storyteller', she couldn't reconcile it with her academic background and calmed her unease by saying that "Stories are just data with a soul." However, anyone who heard Brown speak knew from the first second that this academic was a natural storyteller and belonged on a stage.

Her TED Talk was posted online, and the views skyrocketed. Brené's TED Talk on the power of vulnerability is in the top five of the most-watched TED Talks in the world, with over 60 million views. Since then, she has published six number 1 *New York Times* bestsellers, which have been translated into more than 30 languages. She is the host of two award-winning podcasts, *Unlocking Us* and *Dare to Lead*.

Brené is the first researcher to have a filmed lecture on Netflix, and in March 2022, she launched a new show on HBO Max focusing on her latest book, *Atlas of the Heart*.

Go viral on social media

In 2016, clinical psychologist and now emeritus professor of psychology at the University of Toronto, Jordan Peterson, posted a series of videos on his YouTube channel criticising the amendment to the Canadian Human Rights Act and the Criminal Code (Bill C-16). The Canadian Parliament intended to introduce 'gender identity and expression' as prohibited grounds for discrimination.

Peterson claimed that Bill C-16 would make the use of certain gender pronouns "compulsory speech", infringing on freedom of speech/expression. He linked this argument to a broader critique of political correctness and identity politics.

His video "Professor against political correctness" went viral and sparked an international media storm. Two years later, Peterson published *12 Rules for Life*, turning him into an internationally sought-after intellectual with controversial views. For his Beyond Order tour in 2023, you could listen to him in concert venues like Ahoy in Rotterdam (8,000 seats).

Nothing happens 'overnight'

Christopher Isaac 'Biz' Stone, co-founder of Twitter (now X), once said:

> ***"Timing, perseverance, and ten years of trying will eventually make you look like an overnight success."***

It may have appeared as an 'overnight success', but it was not. No one becomes successful overnight. It is the result of something you have been working on for years, during which you often unexpectedly make several choices that catapult you much further. Even more so, success is not activated by the entrepreneur, the artist, or the academic, but by the market that suddenly becomes aware of the value.

> After all, Peterson had already started posting his lectures at Harvard and the University of Toronto online in 2013. He did this on his own YouTube channel, Jordan Peterson Videos. The earliest recordings date back to Harvard lectures in 1996. He had already built an online audience and written a book. Had he not done that, his video expressing his critique of Bill C-16 might never have been noticed. The TED Talks he gave in 2011 and 2013 did not catapult him to international thought leader status, while Brené Brown's in 2010 did so for her.

Like Peterson, Harari also decided to do more with his teaching material. He chose to turn it into a book that became an Israeli bestseller. But the subsequent step – the translation into English under the title *Sapiens* – blasted him into the status of a global thought leader.

Lauren Griffiths, with the opportunities she got from her statement going viral, could have made a career switch and become a public figure, but she did not.

Brown, Peterson, and Harari, three academics, could just as well have chosen 'Stay in your lane' philosophy, as most academics and scientists would. But they chose to make their vision known to a broad, non-academic audience, and to present it in such a way that this audience could understand it and find it engaging. They chose to stand in the spotlight and the wind. And the entrepreneur in them saw that it was smart.

Summary of Chapter 9: Overnight success

4 things to remember:

1. An overnight success never happens overnight.
2. "Timing, perseverance, and ten years of trying will eventually make you look like an overnight success."
3. Success is not activated by the entrepreneur, the artist, or the academic, but by the market that suddenly becomes aware of the value.
4. 3 ways to have overnight success: Write a bestseller, Give a TED Talk, Go viral on social media.

Chapter 10: Process versus status

Not everyone has the potential to become a personality brand or thought leader. It makes no sense to convince people otherwise. While such a dream sells, I prefer to leave that to others. Not everyone is interested in it either, and that's perfectly okay. I've seen it happen so often in the world of arts. There are many more people who dream of becoming a famous actor. I've seen talents fail because they didn't handle their marketing tactically and strategically. I've seen non-talents score and land one deal after another and, fortunately, I also know actors who could do both. But here's the thing: there's status and there's the process. In language, it's easy to distinguish because the first is a noun: personal brand, and the other a verb: personal branding.

The process is the conscious and deliberate effort to create and influence the public perception of an individual (the What) by enhancing their credibility and distinguishing themselves from the competition (the How).

The goal is to ultimately advance their career or business, expand their circle of influence, and have a greater impact (the Why). The higher your level of influence is, the bigger your status as you can see in the picture.

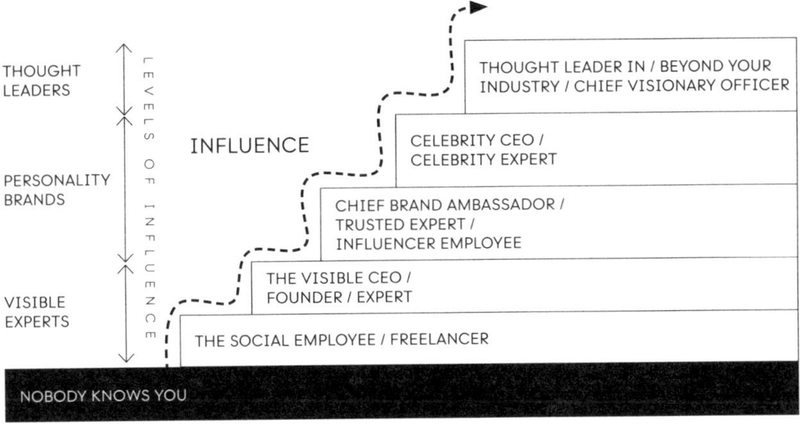

Not everyone can have the status of a personality brand, but everyone can engage in the process of personal branding and benefit from it. Even more so, in today's market, I would advise you to do so if you do not plan to stay with the same employer for your whole life, aspire to run more than one company, for instance, or want to differentiate yourself from other experts. Everyone can achieve the status of an online Visible Expert. If your ambition is higher, the process can also position you as the authority in a field.

The extent to which you are considered an authority depends on various factors that I will discuss later. What I want to share with you first are the different levels in the process that I have seen recur in my career across very different industries and which I also find reflected in the professional literature I have consulted during my research.

There are three levels in the personality branding process. The first is that of the Visible Experts, then you have the Personality Brands, and finally, the Thought Leaders. A level has two growth phases starting with an entry level and then progressing to the next level. Each phase has its own status. For each status the impact on your life, your work, and your environment is different, as is the influence you can exert.

With every status I mention, you'll find different 'profiles' like employees, expert-solopreneurs, founders and executives. That's because the process is different for those who are their own boss, are employees or have high responsibilities in the company they work for.

Level 1: Visible Experts

Status:
- Social employee/freelancer
- Visible Expert
- Visible CEO/founder

If there's one level in the process of personal branding that you really should achieve, it's the level of the Visible Experts. Why else would you create an account on a platform like LinkedIn? To watch others? To build a network while not showing anything about yourself? If this is the case, you belong to the Nobody Knows You group. It's a category that the majority of LinkedIn users fall into. A category on LinkedIn characterised by:
- the absence of a banner and/or profile photo;
- an 'about me' section that is not, or is barely, filled out and lacks available contact details;
- the most recent post being three months old;
- posts that are only reposts from others;
- profiles that are activated when looking for a job or when a vacancy arises.

Visible Expert is the first level in the personality branding process that you can achieve. It mainly takes place online and involves actively using a professional platform like LinkedIn. This means publishing a weekly post and ensuring that you utilise the features LinkedIn offers as effectively as possible. Examples of these are your banner, your 'about me' section, the 'featured' section, your contact details, and your work experience.

When you publish a post, it is not a repost from someone else, but something you have written yourself that reflects your personality and your professional interests and expertise. In addition, you also respond to posts from others in your feed by leaving valuable comments. And you start following other members and connect with them.

If you maintain this consistently, you will notice a significant difference in your visibility after a year. When you read the profile and activity feed of a Visible Expert, you get a good sense of this person. You gain insight into their personality, how they thrive in their professional environment, you learn about the company they work for, and you visualise it.

> A client of mine, the founder of a small law firm specialising in a niche area of law, had very little time to engage with posting on LinkedIn. He found it odd as a lawyer, didn't know what he should talk about, and feared criticism. He didn't see the benefit of it because he was "up to his ears in work".
>
> Yet, he gave it a chance. After just eight posts, it paid off: he not only gained new but also bigger clients. To respond to this, we immediately started working on reorganising his 'CEO schedule', his revenue model, and how he should manage his time. It made clear to him that his visibility on a platform like LinkedIn generated revenue and that it was worth his time and energy.
>
> My client has no ambition to become a personality brand or thought leader, but being a visible expert has already yielded significant benefits for him. A year later, he has doubled his rates, expanded his office, purchased a building, and hired extra staff.

If you're a solo entrepreneur (freelancer, expert), becoming a visible expert should naturally be your goal. A platform like LinkedIn is ideally suited for finding B2B clients, where you can expand your professional network to such an extent that you can work internationally. Because you work solo, your company brand and your personal brand are more intertwined in the same profile. This has its advantages and disadvantages. Many Visible Experts can be recognised by posts in which they share tips and tricks.

Do you want to position yourself as an expert or as a freelancer? There's a difference between the two. For a freelancer, it's sufficient to become a social freelancer, where visibility and general skill representation on platforms like LinkedIn may suffice. From an expert, however, more distinctive capability and expertise are expected, and becoming a Visible Expert is the minimum. The content they share will also differ accordingly.

Why should you become a social employee if you are an employee?

This is interesting for recruiters who are looking for you. According to LinkedIn research, every minute eight people find a job via LinkedIn, and every second 101 job vacancies are added. In their search for talent, recruiters look at your profile and feed to discover who you are and if you might be suitable.

If you decide to become a social employee, you increase your chances of receiving new job offers and yes, even a higher salary. Because employees with a strong profile and good visibility also enhance the attractiveness of the employer.

You might wonder what is better: showing nothing and wanting to keep everything for the conversation itself (if you get one, that is), or a good active profile that already gives them a good idea?

What does the Visible Expert mean for a CEO, executive, or leader?

The same as it means for an employee, but in reverse. Employees want to discover what kind of boss they will be working for. You already read about this extensively in a previous chapter. For a CEO, becoming a Visible CEO is an absolute must. If you want to avoid having to do reputation management and having to act when things go wrong, it's better to prevent things from going wrong in the first place. And this is by building your own 'owned media'. And by already being present on channels so that you have a reach to be able to counteract any headwinds.

Celebrities have been doing this for a long time when it comes to their most important and personal stories. A pregnancy, an illness, a birth... they are tired of seeing the news hijacked by paparazzi who make a gross profit from it and moreover twist the truth to their advantage. But also, sharing important news first on your own channels and then possibly through the press can also come across as more sympathetic and credible.

Being a Visible CEO is still a safe place. You are present, offering quality content, but you don't ask for too much attention.

Level 2: Personality Brands

Status:

- Influencer employee
- Chief Brand Ambassador/Trusted Expert/ Celebrity CEO/Celebrity Expert

From this level onwards, your personality branding process really starts to bear fruit. However, the stakes are higher. Personality Brands have at least tripled their online activity. Think about posting multiple times a week, reaching thousands, tens of thousands, or even hundreds of thousands of followers. The quality of the posts is higher, there is a higher number of reactions, and there are also business opportunities.

They are also present and visible offline in other people's networks (PR). Personality Brands are regularly asked to be guests on podcasts, programmes, or as speakers at events. Due to their increased market value, they can drastically increase their fees.

On the flip side is the work required to maintain and strengthen that status. Just posting on LinkedIn is no longer sufficient; content must also be available in other ways, with deeper insights expected.

The status of a personality brand is maintained by the grace of your market value and how popular you are. Working on your personality, your body of work, and your magnum opus will help you remain congruent with who you are and what you stand for when external pressure becomes too great. But also, to continue providing value.

I wish that every employee could have a CEO who has achieved the status of the Chief Brand Ambassador. What a fantastic experience it must be to have a boss who publicly is the biggest fan of their company, its products, its employees, and the work culture.

I'll go even further by saying that you should only start with employer branding when you have a Visible CEO who has evolved into a Chief Brand Ambassador. Specifically, this means, for example, that they walk the talk in every spot, every advertisement that goes out to attract new talent.

A Chief Brand Ambassador is not 'discreetly' present on LinkedIn but is a fan, an evangelist, and will always and everywhere loudly and clearly proclaim their optimism and vision. As a CBA, you gain loyal followers, employees, and build a positive network.

As an expert, you have now achieved the status of the go-to expert, the Trusted Expert who is called first by the media when an opinion is needed. Your expertise is known and appreciated, your reach has noticeably expanded beyond your customer base and close network. This shows in the size of your LinkedIn network or other social media channels you actively maintain.

As an Influencer Employee, you have built a network outside of your work where you have an impact. Combine that with enthusiastic brand ambassadorship for your employer, and you have struck gold. Then you are indeed a significant asset to your employer precisely because you also have a voice as an individual. Your reach extends beyond your inner circle of colleagues, and you are building recognition outside your own workplace. This can work against you if you have a jealous employer but equally in your favour if your employer recognises that you tap into networks where there may also be opportunities for the company. It can earn you a higher salary, a promotion, or ... other jobs.

PODCAST ALERT
In my podcast Own Your Story, I engage in conversations with Influencer Employees and **Chief Brand Ambassadors.**

Entering the level of Personality Brands, you surpass the Visible Experts in terms of expertise and visibility. Specifically, this means being visible online multiple times a week, delivering keynotes within companies and at events of third parties, being invited as a guest on podcasts, and in explanatory programmes. You are actively engaged in not only achieving but also maintaining this status. Creating content is a fixed part of your schedule. Content-wise, you will also go further than in the previous stage.

Moving forward within personality brands, you'll become the Celebrity CEO and Celebrity Expert. This is an even more well-known version than the first. Merely mentioning the name already rings a bell, even in other industries. Just as there are celebrities in music and film, there are also celebrities in a business environment. Even though they possess a similar level of expertise as the entry level of Personality Brands, their market value is higher. Often, this is because their charisma is greater, their network provides more support, and they make better business decisions. In a corporate company culture, a Celebrity CEO is viewed with suspicion. There's even a preference to avoid having their CEO become a celebrity. Understandably, things can easily go wrong. If the CEO makes a misstep or steps back, it could impact the company. But whether you become a Celebrity CEO is not always within your control. You can dial it back, but ultimately, the public chooses its stars.

The same applies to experts. If your ambition is to become a Celebrity Expert, you need a robust marketing machine. Rigorous consistency, high frequency, and extensive content creation are a must. But if you do all this for an audience that doesn't want it, you'll fail. If it does work, you can count on a lot of media attention, keynote speaking opportunities, and interesting partnerships, as well as much higher fees. A pitfall, however, is that celebrity status for most is not sustainable and only lasts until the next new famous expert comes along.

Level 3: Thought Leadership

Status:

- Chief Visionary Officer
- Thought Leader in/beyond your industry

If you aim for a more sustainable and high status in personality branding, then that would be the status of a Thought Leader. Much digital ink has been spilled over thought leadership. In the rush to distinguish oneself from others, there isn't much left on the market after becoming a go-to expert other than to name oneself a thought leader. 1,260,000 professionals mention Thought Leader in their LinkedIn bio. This title seems logical when seduced by the frenzy of numbers. With 30K or more followers on LinkedIn, with exorbitant amounts you can charge for speaking engagements, with 'everyone' knowing you and referring to your work, it quickly seems like you must be a thought leader. However, fame is something different from thought leadership.

I'm not your thought leader

> When I spoke to Peter Hinssen about this book and mentioned that he was a thought leader, he immediately dismissed the idea. I was taken aback. "Who do you consider a thought leader, then?" I asked him. John Hagel, he replied. I found that interesting.

Peter is a renowned keynote speaker, author, serial entrepreneur, and investor. He is a sought-after thought leader on radical innovation and the impact of technology on society and business. And yet he directed me to another thought leader. Other (Flemish) international speakers who are called thought leaders by others also immediately say they are not. Rik Vera calls himself a thinker, a business philosopher. Pascal Coppens, also a partner at Nexxworks and a China expert, preferred the term Thought Provoker. And that term, for me, most accurately covers the essence.

PODCAST ALERT

Listen to the conversations I have with thought leaders.

In my post on LinkedIn where I mentioned how many professionals call themselves a thought leader or expert, a series of cynical-sounding comments followed. Notably, they were all Flemish voices, while I hear different opinions in American circles. The perceptions of thought leadership and the status of a thought leader are highly dependent on your personal stance, the culture you live in, the sector you work in, and your level of knowledge.

It's not 'bon ton' to call yourself a thought leader. But when others bestow the title upon you, I see two things happening: you strike while the iron is hot and leverage it by sharing it on your socials. And let the lever effect do its work. That's what most people do.

Another strategy is to publicly declare that you are not one. That's what life and business strategist Tony Robbins, known for his self-help books and mega-events, did by titling his 2016 Netflix documentary *I'm not your guru*.

A beautiful example of how, in denying a claim, you can still frame the assertion and claim it for yourself without coming across as arrogant, as in this case. Sounds confusing? Let me explain further. By saying "I'm not your guru", you suggest humility, stay grounded, and protect yourself from criticism of presumed arrogance. In reality, you're framing it in such a way that people still link you to a guru status. This is a well-known technique used extensively in journalism and politics, of which you may not always be aware. Both strategies ensure that you remain uninvolved and thus essentially soothe your conscience while still benefiting from the situation.

Is there another way to deal with it? Yes there is. If someone calls you a thought leader, then publicly thank them and feel honoured. But beyond that, you neither deny, encourage, nor argue. Then, you get back to work, because the real work of a thought leader is never done. Staying ahead in thinking, building bridges, and seeing what others do not see is a never-ending story.

After all, you're not automatically a thought leader because you're the most well-known expert in your knowledge area, such as LinkedIn. You don't just become a thought leader because you've written ten books and delivered 1,000 keynotes on your expertise. Similarly, you're not a thought leader just because you publish the results of research you've funded, or because you've taken a course in trend watching.

Marketers and experts often turn thought leadership into an (online) content strategy where you position yourself as an authority in the market and express opinions publicly. However, being an opinion leader is still different from being a thought leader.

I've spent a long time contemplating what exactly makes thought leadership distinct. I've read through virtual libraries and, in my work as a moderator, have met countless speakers, some of whom are genuine thought leaders. And there is indeed a difference.

First and foremost, I distinguish between corporate thought leadership and individual thought leadership. Why? Because the professional literature mainly discusses the former. Companies like McKinsey, Deloitte, Salesforce, KPMG, Accenture, and CapGemini invest significant budgets in developing thought leadership. The strategies and frameworks described in the professional literature are not comparable to how individual thought leadership comes about.

The reference to individual thought leadership in Laurie Young's work describes a strategy that is far too light. Following this could indeed allow almost any expert to call themselves a thought leader.

So, what is it then (for and according to me)?

Thought leaders (or rather: thought provokers) are a distinct breed. What sets them apart from all other categories is not the tactics. Others also write books, deliver keynotes, publish a lot of content, engage in podcasting, and so on. What distinguishes them from Trusted Experts and Celebrity Experts is:

- The quality of their thinking and its diversity
- A very pronounced novel point of view
- Indifference to criticism
- Challenging the status quo
- An endless curiosity and eagerness to learn
- Their capacity to develop long-term visions
- The ability to look at things both in detail and from a helicopter view
- The ability to formulate questions before they become relevant
- The skill to balance opportunity against danger
- Connecting dots that others have yet to see.

With these traits, they get to work to articulate and make their ideas accessible to the masses. When you become a thought leader, developing insights and sharing them in various types of content and formats becomes your profession. Doing this can change the thinking of individuals, groups, and industries. The subtitle of Laurie Young's book on thought leadership encapsulates for me what it should be: "Prompting businesses to think and learn". That is what an (individual) thought leader should provoke.

Own your name, or someone else will

A thought leader in the knowledge economy is like Pippi Longstocking – charismatic and irritating at the same time. She does her own thing and believes, "I have never tried that before, so I think I should definitely be able to do that." She always turns the status quo on its head.

What about thought leaders like Elon Musk? He doesn't occupy himself with writing and delivering keynotes, does he? Obviously not. He is a Chief Visionary Officer. The CEO version of a TL (Thought Leader). He translates his visionary vision into actions, into products. Or should I rather call him the reincarnation of Pippi Longstocking?

You won't find a thought leader employee. When you've reached that point in your career, you no longer have the ambition to be an employee.

So, there are several levels and statuses in personal branding. And you decide for yourself which status you want to pursue. Your first task is to figure out at which of these levels you are currently. Then, you need to decide which level you want to achieve. Before you leap directly to thought leader, keep in mind that each subsequent step requires more effort and time than the one below it. Are you ambitious and dedicated enough to make it happen? Only you can answer that.

Own your name

One of the very first steps you can take in your personal branding process is a very simple one: make sure your name belongs to you. This book has been titled *Own Your Story. Or Someone Else Will*. But the same applies to your name.

> ***Own your name, or someone else will.***

When I see on Instagram that one of my fellow actors has announced another fake profile, and then hear from my clients that they don't have a URL with their own name, I realise the extremes I'm dealing with.

In real life, you have a house where you live. But you also need an online 'home'. A place where you decide on the content, actions, and visuals. A place that is connected to what is most personal to you: your name and personality. It's surprising how many leaders, founders, and employees have accounts on various social media channels but no online hub in their name that connects them.

If you want to engage in personal branding, then you must ensure that search engines not only find you but also that they lead to your own channels. Go ahead and Google yourself. Which links appear on the first page? Is it your LinkedIn profile? Perhaps a link to a Facebook page, or a publication in a magazine? The company you work for? Or just that namesake of yours? All these online places are not yours, and you don't control or direct the conversation and information there. Start your personal branding process by creating your personal online hub. Own your name. Purchase the domain name with your personal name. If necessary, put this book down now and do it. Please. Thank me later in a DM.

If you don't see why you should have this, I'll give you a few good reasons. You create a personal and professional brand identity over which you have control and ownership. You decide the content, the look, the experience yourself. It also offers flexibility if your career path changes. Your personal domain name serves as a central hub that connects all your online platforms, making it easier for people to find you, remember you, and get in touch with you.

Do you understand why owning your personal domain name is a crucial step at the beginning of your personal branding process? It should be an easy action to buy a domain name that matches your name, but often it's not. When your name is a Jane Doe name, there's a good chance another Jane Doe has already claimed the .com.

Here are some tips for choosing the right domain name:

a. Keep it simple: Choose a version of your personal domain name that is easy to spell, pronounce, and remember. Avoid using hyphens, numbers, or unusual characters that could make your domain confusing or complicated.

b. Use your full name or a variation that accurately represents your personal name.

c. Consider domain extensions: While .com is the most common domain extension, you can also explore other options like .me, .name, or country-specific extensions (.be, .us, .co.uk) if they align with your goals.

d. Check availability and trademarks: Perform a domain name search to check if the name you want is available. Also, research trademarks or existing brands that might conflict with your domain name.

e. Think long-term when choosing a domain name. Avoid trendy or time-sensitive terms that may become outdated. Avoid using a job title.

Make the domain name lead somewhere, even if it's not to your website. Many people think that once they've purchased a domain name, they need to launch a fully designed website right away. But that's not the case. There are very accessible and inexpensive — even free — alternatives you can use until you have the time and budget to develop a personal website. What you should do (in order of ease) is the following:

1. Forward the domain name to, for example, your LinkedIn profile. When utilised well, this platform can become your best-converting website.

2. Open an account with Link-in-bio software and link your domain to it. In this Link-in-bio, you can list various other online hubs you own. You often see this on Instagram profiles.

3. Create a one-pager website with basic info and link it to your domain name.

These three options can take between 10 minutes and half a day's work.

Summary of Chapter 10: Process versus status

9 things to remember:

1. The personal branding process is the conscious and deliberate effort to create and influence the public perception of an individual (what) by enhancing their credibility and distinguishing themselves from the competition (how), ultimately to advance their career or business, expand their circle of influence, and have a greater impact (why).
2. Know the difference between the personal branding process and its statuses.
3. Engaging in the process will benefit everyone; getting a status is a deliberate choice.
4. Every status comes with a price.
5. Assess your online presence: which zone are you in?
6. Get out of the Nobody Knows You Zone.
7. The minimum goal should be the Visible Expert level.
8. Find out what status you want to achieve and if you are willing to put in the effort.
9. Owning your name is step one. Make sure you claim your name on your social media profiles, and domain name.

Chapter 11: The three dimensions of personality branding

If personality branding is the conscious and deliberate effort to create and influence the public perception of you as an individual by enhancing your credibility and distinguishing yourself from the competition, then you do so through your actions and communication. Actions are not visible to outsiders when they are not communicated about. That's why personality branding cannot exist without content creation. But despite what most people think, that content creation does not thrive only online.

Personal branding operates in three dimensions: online, in real life and virtual. The dimensions certainly overlap but also have their own set of rules. Finding your sweet spot is becoming congruent, consistent and valuable in all three. This will strengthen your status even more.

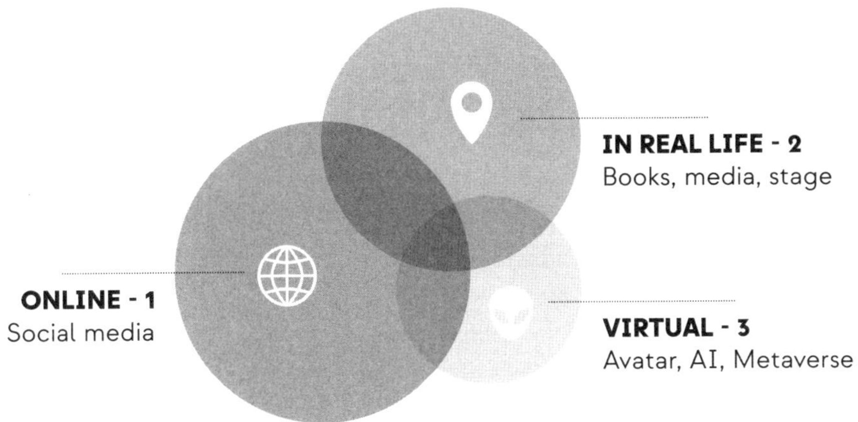

The three dimensions of personality branding.
Congruency lives in the interaction of all three.

Traits of a master communicator

No matter in what dimension you are actively building your personality brand, you must become a master communicator if you want to achieve status. Becoming a master communicator is crucial in personality branding. Luckily the same key skills are needed across all three dimensions and various platforms:

Storytelling: Regardless of the platform, storytelling is an essential skill. It's about engaging your audience with your journey, your vision, and your values. A good story captivates, inspires, and resonates. Whether you're writing a book, delivering a keynote, or creating posts on social media, mastering the art of storytelling can help you convey your personality brand in an engaging way. We've already discussed developing your key narratives in the chapter on narrative development. But this technique will also be necessary in online/offline content creation, PR, and sales.

Content creation: Creating engaging, valuable content is key to communicating your personal brand. This can be writing (for blogs, books, social media posts), audio/video production (for podcasts, YouTube videos), or visual design (for infographics, photos). Good content should reflect your unique voice and perspective.

Public speaking: For keynotes or podcasts, speaking skills are essential. You need to be able to articulate your thoughts clearly, engage your audience, use your voice effectively, and manage nerves.

Digital literacy: In today's digital age, understanding how various online platforms work is crucial. Each platform has its own 'language' – certain types of content, tones, and styles work better on certain platforms. Tailoring your message to the platform can increase its reach and impact.

Congruence: While not a skill per se, authenticity is vital in personality branding. People connect with genuineness. Let your true self shine through your content, your speeches, your imagery. This congruence will make your personal brand more discoverable and impactful.

Strategic thinking: Strategic thinking is important in deciding how, where, and when to communicate your brand. You need to understand your audience, your platform, your message, and how your personality brand aligns.

Consistency in your message and voice helps to strengthen and reinforce your personal brand. Consistent brand recognition tells your audience what to expect from you and builds trust and recognition.

Remember, you can develop and refine these skills over time. It's a process, remember?

Summary of Chapter 11: The three dimensions of personality branding

4 things to remember:

1. The online dimension is used the most to build your brand; it is also the easiest to grow.
2. In real life is the dimension most used in corporate life and for Gen X, and for those who achieved status online.
3. The virtual dimension is yet to come, but it sure is promising.
4. In all three dimensions you need to become a master communicator if you pursue status. The same traits are needed.

Chapter 12: Tactics for online personality branding

Online personality branding is the easiest to start, and it's the most talked about on social media and in sales training. Due to the democratisation of tools that allow you to make your voice heard, anyone can build their own media company in an accessible and affordable way. All you need is a recent smartphone and a few apps. That's it. With these, you can essentially do everything: write, record, film, edit, publish, ...

When you embark on online personality branding, you can spend your days learning and improving a plethora of skills and tools that will be useful to you. There are so many possibilities that without a strategy and focus, you might lose yourself and give up before you even start. There is an explosion of software tools, platforms, and available media you can use to make yourself visible. How do you find your way in this paradise of growth opportunities?

In this chapter, I want to provide insight into the tactics available and, as a curator, chart a path for you that I hope deviates from your usual path so that you can look at it in a different way. This can help in making decisions. So first, a brief and concise overview of the key ingredients from which you will make a choice:

1. There are two **ways** to communicate: speaking or writing.
2. There are four **actions** you can perform to communicate: create, document, repurpose, and interact.
3. Each action must be put into one or more content **formats**.
4. A format has a certain narrative **structure**. This could be, for example: blog, conversation, article, quote, ...

5. You can choose a **length**: long-form, short-form.
6. And you can also choose a **communication style**: inspiring, provocative, educational, entertaining, ... Or you can make multiple combinations.
7. A carrier of content is the **medium** you choose to communicate, such as paper, digital, image, or audio.

A content carrier needs a **distribution channel** through which it can be spread and your audience can find it. Bookstore, YouTube, LinkedIn, Spotify.

Let's now delve into each of them.

Speaking or writing?

There are two ways you can communicate: through speaking or writing. This is possibly the most important decision you need to make first, and one that nobody alerts you to. You are not equally good and fast at both things. You might think you are, but that's not the case. One of the two communication methods suits you better than the other. And by better, I mean: it yields a better result more quickly.

Many people consider themselves better speakers than writers. However, what many don't realise about themselves is whether what they communicate and how is interesting. Many people can indeed "fill the air with sound" and conclude from this that they are also smooth speakers. In reality, the content they deliver is of little value, they use a lot of filler words, and they often ramble on with generalities.

If you are someone who prefers speaking over writing, then prepare what you are going to say on paper, so you think ahead and reflect on what you are going to say.

There is also a group that prefers writing to speaking. Often the reason is that they can be more thoughtful about what is being said. Attention to nuance, to meaning, to tone of voice, to language, and style.

The pitfall for this group lies in written language that is so stiff that it becomes unattractive.

Are you someone who prefers writing over speaking? Then work on using spoken language in your writing. How do you do that? Well: run through what you want to say in your head and write it down like that. Then read it out loud several times. Written language is not easily spoken.

When you want to achieve speed and volume in your content creation, it is important to choose a form of communication that you are both good at and fast. Of course, you can work on this and improve.

In my opinion, speaking is the most valuable. Why? Because when we see you speak, we can experience the most of you. We experience your presence, your body language, your facial expressions, your voice, your intonation, your choice of words, your content, your emotions. It doesn't get more all-encompassing than that. Moreover, you can always create a written version of your talk afterward. And there's another reason. When you start building a content creation machine, recording a video of you speaking is the best and most efficient move. More on that later.

Choose an action

There are four types of actions in content creation that you can undertake. The actions differ from each other in the intensity of the work expected from you.

1. **Expert content creation:** Here, you work with your own insights and develop an idea, learning, or anything else into a completely self-created piece of content. This is material that you can repurpose several times over a long period. You make it evergreen. Example: you develop a question you received from a client into an article, you write an e-book about XYZ.

2. **Documenting:** Think of reality TV. Here, you use your activities as the subject for content creation. This is the easiest form of content creation because it simply means looking at your schedule, choosing what might be interesting for your audience and posting about it. For example: you film your keynote, you take photos of the conference you visit... If you're smart, you make sure your recorded material isn't too specific in terms of date and location. Then you can reuse it multiple times. Gary Vaynerchuk is king in documenting his working life. He shamelessly reuses videos from ten years ago to prove he was right.

3. **Share:** You use someone else's content or your company's content for your own personal brand. This is so easy that it's the most misused content that actually doesn't add value to your personal branding. And yet, it can be used well, but not by using the 'share/repost' button. How do you use it correctly? By processing the information in a post where you give your own opinion on the subject and refer to the original article. Example: you are inspired by a report you read, and you write a post about it. This is often content that is not reusable. And that's okay.

4. **Engage:** An action many forget is to interact with your network, your followers, and the people you find interesting to follow. A personal brand needs an audience, a network, a community. Does this have to take up a lot of your time? No. If you engage with your audience and comment on their posts around the time you publish your own post, then it's a win-win for your own reach.

These actions can be used on different media: you can use them on your social media channel, but just as well when writing a book, giving a keynote, or an interview for a podcast. Engaging in these four actions gives people a quicker sense of you as a personality because it shows you on different levels. Do the test yourself and see who among the people you follow is differentiated enough in their approach. You will notice that usually one action is chosen. And do not confuse an action with a carrier.

Put the action into a content format

A format has a specific narrative structure, such as a blog, conversation, article, quote, etc. Along with this, you can choose a length: long-form, short-form. And also a style: inspiring, provocative, educational, entertaining, ...

When you decide to undertake a specific action, you have multiple choices to shape that action. You can also develop multiple choices and reuse the action several times.

For example, you want to create a piece about an insight you've gained. You aim to inspire others (style), you decide to write a blog post about it (format), not too long (short form). Then you realise there are a few great quotes in it that you could use as a tweet or Instagram quote (format).

You can plan and determine all this in advance, but it can also happen organically. Depending on your experience and skills, you choose one over the other. Above all, give yourself the freedom to experiment. Too often, I notice that locking everything into methodologies and action plans works counter-productively.

Writing, just like speaking, is a crucial skill when you aspire to be a personality brand and thought leader. Like speaking, it requires a lot of practice and the freedom to experiment. Being able to write without it causing stress is bliss. It strengthens your thinking, your language skills, your emotional intelligence.

I find it more important to do first before learning. When I work with clients on their keynote, I make them write it first. For some, this triggers panic. They don't understand that in their request to be coached in writing and delivering a keynote, they first need to write it. For them, it seems like I'm throwing them into the deep end and letting them drown before teaching them to swim. What they don't realise is that if I were to teach them the technique of writing a keynote first, they wouldn't put on the 'creator's hat' but that of the editor. They wouldn't get a single letter down on paper. You learn much more from analysing what you can and adjusting what could be done differently.

Moreover, that first draft provides me with a treasure trove of information about them, information they often don't realise themselves. Through my experience with scenarios, I can deduce from their writing style how they handle information, how they deal with language, how their thoughts leap, how they use structure, whether they use storytelling, humour, etc. I learn what potential they have within them, malformed habits, their level of thinking. After reading, I can get to work on adjusting where necessary, teaching what's missing, nurturing what's still small, and cutting out what hurts. It yields a faster, much better, and more beautiful result than starting with the theory lesson 'how to write XYZ'. I do the same with podcasting, video, interviews, content writing. Learning by doing.

Choose a content carrier or medium

A content carrier needs a distribution channel or a platform so your audience can find it. Think of bookstores, YouTube, LinkedIn, Spotify.

Your choice between writing or speaking immediately decides the carrier for your piece of content. Although you can always take 'a detour' by first writing out your podcast or video script and then recording it. Personally, I don't consider that much of a detour, but of course, I am trained to work from a written text.

Once you've placed your piece on a carrier, you can choose which distribution platform to use. The choice might require some extra work to truly tailor it to the preferences of that platform. A TikTok video is created differently from a video meant for LinkedIn. Although you'll see the line between the two start to blur. Argh.

Creating valuable content in the formats of a platform can feel like wearing two hats at the same time, which is a step too far for most experts. Hence my creed to first create value and then to rework it into a format that fits the distribution channel until you become good and fast at it and you are able to combine the two. You want to become a personality brand, find your own voice, not just be a plaything of a distribution platform?

Distribution channels have become savvy at immersing a combination of what you just read in their own brand language, overwhelming us with jargon like YouTube videos, short videos, Reels, Stories, IG, Tweets, podcasts, e-books, Facebook Live, etc. You soon get the impression that you need to be present on all those platforms. That the grass on that other platform is just a tad greener.

If you have a team and a budget available, you can go all the way, if that's what will benefit you the most. It makes no sense to invest time and money in a platform where there's nothing for you to gain. Are you like most of us, limited, or don't want to spread yourself thin like Nutella on white bread? Then opt for one main platform and one or two sub-platforms. Your main platform is the one where you invest most of your time and energy for strategic reasons. Your sub-platforms are backups. You're present, maybe a bit less active, but they can still find you there. If you ever get thrown off or hacked from one, you won't be left empty-handed.

The content creation process

Faced with so many choices, it's easy to feel overwhelmed. Let's try to look at content creation from a different angle and discover that it can be divided into three phases: content development, content production, and content distribution.

Content development

Do you want to position yourself as an expert? A thought leader? Then ensure that what you communicate comes from your brain (and not from an AI). Your vision, your way of looking at things, your insights and opinions, your techniques, your opinion... As a personality brand, it's important to create value for your target audience. And this value must also clearly contain your personal added value. Specifically, this means that your distinguishing factor is clearly noticeable. So, if you're going to work with content writers who create your posts, or want to use generative AI, develop the reflex to work from your distinguishing factor and guide both accordingly.

Content production

You know what you want to create content about? Now it's time to produce it. You are (for now) indispensable when the production involves video or audio. I say for now, because the rapid evolution, and especially the democratisation of AI tools, will also ensure that both your voice and likeness can be perfectly and naturally executed by an AI. Whether that will have the same impact remains a question. But until then, you're needed to stand in front of a camera or microphone. Anything that can be written down can be done by software or freelancers.

PODCAST ALERT
Listen to episodes where I speak with AI users and experts.

Content distribution

For this phase in content creation, you're actually not needed at all. This can be completely done by others, or if you want to do it yourself, made less time-intensive by using an automation tool.

Now that you've learned to see the mountain called content creation as stages in climbing, each with its own basecamp, I want to show you some mechanisms by which you can make your content creation work like a machine. Work smarter, not harder.

Summary of Chapter 12:
The tactics in online personal branding

A lot to remember! Get a grip on all the possibilities in creating an online brand by knowing the basics:

1. There are two ways to communicate: speaking or writing.
2. There are four actions: create, document, repurpose, and interact.
3. Every action must be put into a content format.
4. A format has a certain narrative structure. This could be, for example: blog, conversation, article, quote, ...
5. You can choose a length: long-form, short-form.
6. And also a communication style: inspiring, provocative, educational, entertaining, ... Or you can do multiple combinations.
7. Choose a medium to communicate, such as paper, digital, image, or audio. Still overwhelmed? Then look at the content creation process as a three step process: 1. Content development (finding ideas, developing content) 2. Content production (turning it into something you can read, hear or look at) 3. Content distribution (putting it online). Now mix and match as you like!

Chapter 13: Do more with less

Master storyteller Raymond Queneau

The godfather of reusing the same piece of content can be found in French literature. Raymond Queneau (1903–1976) was a French novelist, poet, and playwright.

After obtaining his Baccalaureate, he moved to Paris to study philosophy at the Sorbonne. He began to show interest in languages (Sanskrit, Arabic, and Hebrew) and literature, but also in anthropology, psychoanalysis, mathematics, and religion. In 1924, Raymond Queneau briefly joined the Surrealists. He started writing in 1930. Queneau worked for most of his life at the renowned French publishing house Gallimard and became the director of one of its collections, l'Encyclopédie de la Pléiade.

I became acquainted with Queneau's work during my drama training. We used his *Exercices de style* (1947) as material to play different interpretations of the same story. *Exercices de style* is one of his most famous works. The book consists of a simple short story retold in 99 different ways. This book is a beautiful example of the richness of storytelling.

This is the story:

In a bus, the narrator encounters a young man with a long neck wearing a hat adorned with a braid instead of a ribbon.

The young traveller exchanges a few heated words with another passenger and then takes a newly vacated seat. Later, the narrator encounters the same young man deeply engaged in conversation with a friend, who advises him to move up the top button of his overcoat.

If you don't understand or feel the impact of your language use in your communication, I advise you to read aloud several versions from *Exercices de style*. You will immediately notice how different elements in your language use determines its impact regarding understanding, emotion, target audience, comprehension.

Queneau loved to experiment in literature. Another experiment was using mathematics as an inspiration for writing. This resulted in a work called *Cent mille milliards de poèmes* (1961). The book is a set of ten sonnets printed on cardstock with each line on a separate strip. Since all ten sonnets not only share the same rhyme scheme but also the same rhyming sounds, all lines from one sonnet can be combined with all lines from the other nine sonnets, making 1014 (= 100,000,000,000,000) different poems possible! The paper edition of the work is a gem and one that I like to pull from my library on autumn days in an attempt to make a sonnet. I am amazed that translators have managed to translate this work into English, German, and Chinese.

Content Creation Machines

An interesting dilemma that often arises is: should you opt for quantity or quality in your content creation? And as always, the answer depends on the commercial goals of the person you're asking. If you ask a marketing agency, they'll say: quantity. Because that's what they can offer. If you ask a content writer who has rebranded as an AI expert? They'll also say quantity because that's precisely the advantage of using generative AI. If you ask a journalist or copywriter? Then the answer is quality. If you ask me, I'd say: Quality is indispensable; quantity depends on your goal and personal preference. Although I also know that quality isn't always the winner in terms of revenue and results.

The chance of making a big impact with one excellently written piece is small. A minimum amount of quantity is needed to become visible. But consistency is more important than frequency. So, it's better to have a consistently lower publication rhythm than to publish a lot at one time and then nothing at all.

Letting the algorithm of a platform determine your strategy is a choice, but I'm not in favour of that myself. What is rewarded by the algorithm one month can be penalised with an adjustment. I take it into account, but that's it.

What's your goal? If you want to be the biggest, then quantity is a must. This ensures that people can't ignore you. Remember that most of your followers won't even see what you publish. However, ensure the quality is good, because high quantity and low quality equals spam and will result in being unfollowed and especially blocked by the platform.

Fortunately, there's a smart way to produce much more without actually creating much more content. It only needs to be 'reworked', which requires less effort and is also easy to outsource. Here lies the solution to much headache for experts: the content creation machine! I'll give you three, there might be others, or you might come up with your ultimate version of one. Be inspired to experiment and then personalise!

Keep-it-simple flow

This content creation machine starts with two conditions: You don't really have a preference for speaking or writing. You also don't have much on your agenda to post about. This is a great flow for professionals aiming for the Visible Expert Level (first level of the personality branding process).

This is the flow:
You decide which 1–3 days of the week you want to post.

- You assign one of the actions to each day. For example, on Monday expert content, on Wednesday document, on Friday share.
- Each time you create a post based on an action, you schedule it for the designated day of the week using LinkedIn's planning tool or other software. The publication happens automatically.

Doing this ensures that you have a consistent presence of at least one post per week and that you build up a stockpile.

Speakers' content creation flow

This is an advanced flow for those aiming for the Trusted Expert level (level 2 in personality branding). This content creation machine starts with the following two conditions: 1. You are a very smooth talker and not a writer, and 2. You have a lot of activities scheduled on your agenda. The basis of this flow is that your main action is documenting.

In other words, all your content creation stems from the recording of a documented moment (macro content).

This is then broken down into micro content that is spread across different formats, carriers, and platforms.

An example: Your schedule includes a keynote at an event in Amsterdam. You go into reality-TV mode and film yourself or get filmed driving there, preparing, giving the keynote, networking afterward. This macro source material is then broken down into many different pieces that could be interesting for your target audience. From one large piece, you could, in principle, provide material for a month. And this even for different social media channels! Gary Vaynerchuk serves as a role model for this flow.

Writers' content creation flow

This is another advanced flow for those aiming for the Trusted Expert level (level 2 in personality branding). This content creation machine starts with the following two conditions: 1. You are a quick writer and not much of a speaker, and 2. You have a greater sensitivity to language and a fluent pen. This flow starts from the action of expert content creation and writing about it.

- You write one macro document weekly. This could be a newsletter, a blog post, an article, or even an e-book.
- From this document, like the previous flow, you create micro content, but you work more with different style versions. You can create lists, a provocative piece, an inspiring piece, a how-to piece, an example, a narrative version, and so on.
- Each piece can refer back to that one large document. You spread the publication over weeks, not days. Weekly, for instance, you could post a version or variant. So, don't go for three variants in the same week as that would be overbearing.

This is a content creation machine that requires higher writing and language skills or... a very good understanding of the use of generative AI as a second brain. Justin Welsh serves as a role model for this machine.

A content creation machine can be outsourced if you have the budget for it. Of course, you can also do it yourself. In that case, take your time, start simple. Persist in the simplest consistency of posting once a week, and grow from there. Don't run before you can walk.

Growing faster with GenAI

Garbage in garbage out

I learned the term "garbage in, garbage out" from former UX strategist Rosemie Callewaert, with whom I founded iStoires, the digital-first publisher of short stories I've talked about before. Rosemie introduced me to the world of UX design during our collaboration. Thanks to her, I started creating websites myself and enjoy trying out new software.

"Garbage in, garbage out," a phrase from computer science and Information Technology, is used to remind people that software and control systems can only provide meaningful information when they are fed with correct information. A computer system, no matter how intelligent, will surely generate nonsensical results if fed with incorrect data.

It's an expression that I also apply in many non-technical situations such as moderating an event, conducting a good interview, or making policy decisions. And now, effortlessly, also in creating content with the help of generative AI.

GIGO is the Achilles' heel of Generative AI on at least two levels:

The first level: the development of AI

The foundation of any effective AI model, especially generative ones, is the data on which it is trained. Feeding an AI system a vast amount of low-quality, biased, or unrepresentative data will inevitably cause the output to reflect these deficiencies. For instance, a language model trained exclusively on classical literature might excel at mimicking Shakespearean prose but falter in understanding modern internet slang.

Biases in training data also lead to outcomes that inadvertently perpetuate harmful stereotypes or misinformation. This is not just a theoretical issue. There have been instances where AI models, after being trained on biased datasets, made decisions that reflected these biases, leading to public outrage and deeper introspection about the ethics of AI.

The second level: developing the prompt

Once a robust AI model has been developed, the responsibility shifts from the developers to you as the user. Herein lies the second level of GIGO vulnerability: the prompt. An AI, no matter how advanced, still operates based on the input it receives. A vague or misleading prompt can result in output that is incorrect, nonsensical, or even outright absurd.

For creative professionals using AI, it's paramount to craft the 'perfect' prompt. To develop prompts like an AI prompt engineer, you should follow a structured approach. The "Who, What, and How" framework is an effective guide to start with.

1. You start by defining the 'Who' by assigning a role or job description to the AI model. Whether it's a copywriter, digital marketer, or even a famous person. By offering their perspective, the role sets the context for the response.
2. The 'What' clearly states the task to be performed. Being specific is crucial. You must leave no room for ambiguity. Unlike a generic Google search, you need to provide a generative AI with precise details so it perfectly understands your requirements.
3. You finish your prompt with the 'How'. Here you dictate the format, tone, and style of the response. Certainly use adjectives that can indicate the desired tone (funny, passionate, business-casual, whimsical, emotional, or assertive). This not only improves the relevance of the results but also their quality. You can also specify the desired format, whether it's a list, spreadsheet, summary, detailed paragraphs, or step-by-step instructions. It further refines the AI's output.

But beyond the "Who, What, and How" framework, there's another distinguishing factor: human intuition, experience, and domain-specific knowledge are needed to obtain qualitative output. And that can only come from you, the questioner.

Asking a generative music AI for "a happy song" could yield very different results than "a cheerful pop song with a catchy chorus reminiscent of chart-toppers from the 2010s". But of course, you need to know that to be able to articulate and ask for it.

Using generative AI in content creation is undeniably interesting to explore and to use as an extension of your thinking, or a second brain.

It offers scalability, speed, and in some cases, unmatched creativity. But as with any tool, its effectiveness depends on how it's used. Understanding and respecting the GIGO principle at both the developmental and operational levels ensures that you can harness the potential of AI without falling prey to its pitfalls. It's essential for both developers and users to remember that a tool is only as good as the hands that wield it and the materials it's given.

Summary of Chapter 13: Do more with less

A few things to remember:

1. Read the work of master storyteller Raymond Queneau, the best example of reusable content.
2. Develop your content creation machine for efficiency.
3. Grow your content production with GenAI but be aware of GIGO.

Chapter 14: Storytelling once more

Discover your storyfield

People are storytellers. Without storytelling, we wouldn't have society, politics, religions, or associations. Stories are necessary to connect large groups of people, to pass on information. Through stories, we can make people remember, motivate them to take action, and convince them.

And everyone, absolutely everyone, carries stories within them. No one escapes experiences in their life that have had an emotional impact and have shaped them. However, the way you deal with those experiences, process them, communicate about them, and the reactions they elicit, will determine whether you are a storyteller or not.

There are people who suppress experiences because they belong to the past. There are people who do not acknowledge and recognise experiences as stories. There are people who dare not present an experience as a story.

In my work as a moderator, public speaking coach, trainer, personal brand builder, but also in my private life, what I do most is eliciting stories from others. By asking questions, probing further, stimulating, and pointing out a story. "This can be turned into content creation," "This is wonderful material for your keynote," "You should definitely use this as the base story for your book," "This story is your essence." When I say this, often unexpectedly and in the middle of a conversation, I see eyes momentarily switch to a questioning look, the brain as a train changing tracks, then seeing the beautiful landscape it arrives in.

You have it in you. It just needs to come out. You need to learn to set up and use your antennae because stories are truly everywhere. What you need to learn is to see the potential. How can you use this story to serve your path?

And don't believe yourself when you think, "I'll remember this story," because that's rarely the case. Note it on your smartphone when you experience something you can use. Record it on your voice recorder and immediately indicate why you think there's potential in what you just told.

Before you start determining what you'll talk about in your content creation, I advise you to go fishing. You're sitting on a pond full of stories; you just haven't seen what kinds of fish are in it yet. Write down the environments you frequent. Are you part of a basketball club? Do you practise yoga? Are you a marathon runner? You're bound to experience things, and chances are you'll meet characters who always have a lot to say. Do you read books, watch movies, listen to music? There's probably something to say that relates to what you do or who you are. Your work, your clients, your suppliers... all stories. And then there's your knowledge. A mush of triviality for you, but a basket full of exotic fruits for those who want to learn. Map this out, fill your pond.

First act, then organise

The likelihood is high that you'll immediately start organising what you want to talk about. You seek clarity, an overview, a plan. And everyone talks about content calendars that clearly outline what you should do, why, and when.

Although this can provide a good sense of control, the real challenge arises when you start implementing that plan. Before you know it, you might find yourself stuck in a kind of content writer's block. All the elements are there, but you can't squeeze out a piece of text. Writing on command sometimes works, other times it doesn't.

Therefore, be gentle with yourself. Don't adhere too strictly to too many rules. Choose which ones you want to follow first and which ones to follow later. For example, posting once a week is the goal. More is allowed, less is not. Don't immediately impose on yourself what you MUST write about. For a while, write about what you feel like, depending on your mood and inspiration. Discover your style. It might not yield much reach, but it might as well.

I've published posts written in one go from a strong emotion. One of them reached 95K views in two days. I didn't think about how it fits with my services or supports my vision. And I've written many more posts that would be considered 'successful' methodologies but yielded nothing. The opposite has happened too.

So, before you cast everything in systems and processes that you must follow like a school child, take a few months to discover yourself as a content creator. Then gradually start adjusting, improving, and strengthening.

Content pillars

When you've been writing for a while, you'll start to gain insight into your style, your go-to themes, and your favourite topics. You'll also start to discover what you're less good at, what you tend to forget. In other words, you gain insight into what already EXISTS. From there, you can continue to build.

You often hear about establishing your content pillars. This generally means creating containers that help in determining relevant content and maintaining an overview in your posting routine.

It's important to realise that you can approach a content pillar in different ways, and many promote a certain approach based on preference.

But actually, that choice depends on how you like to archive and who you work with. If you outsource your content creation, you need to find a system that everyone can think and work with. If you work alone, definitely go for one you feel comfortable with.

Here is an example from a completely different angle: as an actor, I have always worked on projects. People, documents, photos, you name it, are all stored by project on my computer and in my head. A project is like a spider web. So what I do is create a project folder and then subfolders within it. Done.

Then I hire an assistant who doesn't think in terms of projects at all and starts making main folders from the subfolders. After a while, we are following two systems and neither works properly. There's something to be said for both approaches. Mine is very handy in the short term when you're in the midst of it. The other is more useful in the long term and especially more convenient for outsiders.

With content pillars, you face a similar issue. Various approaches are possible. To give a few examples:

- Theme-oriented (leadership, innovation, personal development, ...)
- Topic-oriented (how to X, how to Y, how to Z)
- Goal-oriented (educate, entertain, sell)
- Format-oriented (video, podcast, quote, carousel, ...)

There are plenty of options, and that often makes it difficult to choose. Deciding how you want to proceed will initially give you more clarity and remove your uncertainty but can feel more like a hindrance over time. I always ended up feeling constrained because sharp dividing lines are relative. For instance, I'd write a post where I 'sold' my training but used an inspiring style. Two pillars in one go. Well, where should I categorise that? Plans are all well-intentioned, just like segmenting and categorising. But all too often, it seems to have a Tupperware effect: too many boxes in your cupboard that you don't use. So how do you determine which pillars work for you?

The first differentiator is: do you work alone, or do you work with a team/agency? If you work with an agency, they will likely want to bring you into their content pillar approach. It's easier for someone who isn't in your head. What's more important for you is knowing what you have to say and about what. As long as you feel good about it and the results are good, why bother.

If you're working alone and have to make all the decisions, look again at the type of person you are and don't get carried away by what supposedly should be done. Let yourself be inspired at most so that you get an idea of what's possible. Then look at what suits you best.

The second differentiator is: what do you find most important in maintaining an overview? Maybe you don't want to lose sight of posting enough videos, regardless of the message. Or maybe you don't want to forget that you also want to run your campaign for your services. If you were to incorporate these two examples into your content pillar system, you'd come up with a new combination where you combine format + goal-oriented.

Those pillars should serve you and help you maintain an overview, not block you. I have combined different types of pillar systems that were recommended to me by coaches. In the end, I ditched them and set up one that was especially practical for me and more aligned with how I could turn my content calendar into a routine. For a while, my pillars were the following: consistency on Tuesday and selling on Thursday. Done. I make sure there are four weeks' worth of posts ready for this. Then I fill in the rest of the week with whatever content I want to share. This can fluctuate. One week daily, another week twice. Like real human behaviour. This is me. To put it in terms of Jung's archetypes: there's a maverick and an explorer in me. A Pippi and an Alice. You are free to agree with me or not at all.

Brand pillars are fundamental

While content pillars can provide a structure for content creation, I find the concept of brand pillars to be more intriguing. These are the real pillars on which you build your house. These are the pillars around which you say: I want to be known for these topics. And you read it correctly, topics is plural. When you aim to grow into a personality brand and even into a thought leader later on, it's crucial that you can transcend the status or 'phase' of being a trusted expert on a specific topic.

For instance, you're a Trusted Expert on LinkedIn when you know everything about the platform. How it works, its newest features, its policy. People automatically refer to you with questions.

You become a personality brand when, in addition to that expertise, you also embrace an overarching theme as your own, such as leadership. You then become a thought leader when you leave behind what is currently happening and think ahead about the role and form that leadership and communication will take in a new era.

So, when you name your brand pillars, you first take what you provide services for, an overarching theme related to it, and a third theme of your choice. This last one can be something completely different, adding a surprising element to your brand. You love talking about these themes more than anything.

I want to become the biggest! The Happy Trend Wave

Jump on a trend and go all in. That's what many content writers on LinkedIn have been doing since December 2022 as they started working with generative AI. It was sink or swim. "People don't lose their jobs because of AI, but because of the people who can work with AI," you constantly saw passing by in your feed. Every day, they posted carousels with new prompts, new apps which they generously shared with the public. People joined them in droves, unable to resist such generosity. I often thought of the soccer stickers you could collect by purchasing products and then trade with others at school. What do people even do with all those prompts they got for free?

> However, it went quite well for a number of those content writers. Over time, they created an inexpensive online course teaching how to use ChatGPT. They were invited to podcasts. Their following soared to 100,000 followers, and they were asked to give keynotes all over the world.
>
> When I contacted one of them to invite him for a discussion about this in my podcast, he replied: "I charge as much for a guest appearance in a podcast as I do for giving a keynote." I asked him how much that was, and he said: $5,000. FYI: for Belgian speakers this is a very high speakers fee, and podcasters don't pay for their guests. I told him that preparing a keynote requires work, but podcast guesting doesn't. He replied, astonished, that he was the second-biggest AI expert on LinkedIn. At this moment, his market value is high. And he can indeed ask whatever he wants. He had certainly jumped on the right trend. He went from nobody to a trusted expert in a niche.

And therein lies the pitfall. At this moment, everyone following this path is on the Happy Trend Wave, where sharing their own journey yields high scores. There is no critical reflection on the trend. On the contrary, dismissing ethical concerns and the lack of reflection on the impact are necessary to feed the hype and thus also the popularity of both the credibility of the trend and one's own branding.

That critical reflection is yet to come. And always at the same moment, namely: when there are too many similar stars in the sky and a new distinguishing feature needs to be found. Suddenly, people become critical of the topics sceptics had been talking about from the start. Once you know the movement, you'll start recognising it. From that moment on, you'll look differently at the value that is delivered.

The many other experts who thought Clubhouse would be the next big thing for their personal brand and thought leadership were mistaken. It was the first time I decided to dive into a new medium as an experiment. Although after a week on Clubhouse I felt that it consumed all your time and energy and gave little back, I found it interesting to observe how well-known and unknown people got to work to strengthen their personal brand with it. Suddenly, everyone called themselves a 'Clubhouse moderator', organisers had their own branded room and regular appointments with their audience. It became painfully clear how few managed to properly guide a conversation and keep it interesting, and how important having a good voice was. And yet, you saw the following of some increase significantly; their rooms were always well-attended, and quite a bit of advertising and selling was done.

Dutch entrepreneur Eelco de Boer practically lived on Clubhouse, so to speak. But you could also hear and have a conversation with American A-list actors live just like that. The barrier to getting in touch with your idols disappeared. To me, that did not seem to be a good move in the long run, because I think it would decrease their market value if this were to continue.

I saw how much work, time, and energy people put into the platform, mostly making the platform grow while they gave away a lot on an inefficient channel. Initially, a Clubhouse conversation could not be recorded, rebroadcast, or anything. I quit quickly. I had other things to do. The success of Clubhouse was, as I and many others had predicted, short-lived. Not only were there new competitors from established platforms that already had strong communities and just needed to create the features, but there was also talk of scams in the rooms. But mainly there was a solution for a problem that still had to be found. Clubhouse was a hype that fit perfectly into a period when the world was locked up at home by a raging pandemic. A time when people walked around half-dressed and had zoom fatigue. Where it was nice just to be able to listen without anyone seeing you.

Jumping on a trend is a risky tactic that can make your personal brand and your business boom or crash. It requires full dedication and all your time. If it works, you can cash in on various levels, but you're not out of the danger zone yet. A trend always passes. Always. At some point, it becomes mainstream. It's up to you to be a step or three ahead by that time. And that is often not realised.

Summary of Chapter 14: Storytelling once more

5 things to remember:

1. Take another look at your story field but now from the perspective of regular communication online.
2. Don't be too hard on yourself if you don't have inspiration to create posts.
3. Use content pillars to structure your publishing scheme.
4. Use brand pillars to get clarity on your core messages.
5. Do you want to be a Happy Trend Wave surfer or not?

Chapter 15: The tactics in real life personality branding

The first dimension, online personal branding, is the biggest but not the oldest. The oldest is the second dimension named 'IRL' or 'In Real Life'. It is the dimension you get into when your impact online is growing hard or when you live a corporate life. But that was not always the case.

The stage – The Speaker

TED makes public speaking hot again

> In 2010, when I was asked to join the organising team of the very first TEDx live in Belgium and to host it as well, I immediately said yes. I had only recently come into contact with the TED concept for the first time and was absolutely thrilled. I just found it a pity that the big congress in LA was only for the happy few who could afford such a fee. But then came the TEDx licence that opened the door to the general public. I was full of the TED philosophy, which prioritised the spreading of ideas. The format of a TED Talk and the views that Chris Anderson had on giving keynotes had a major impact on how keynotes were generally given.

Let me share with you the three main innovations:

1. A TED talk articulates an idea worth spreading. In other words, it makes people look at something in a different way and think about it.

2. Then there was the duration of such a talk. Anderson believed that it could not last longer than 18 minutes, as the audience's attention span then waned. He also believed that if you couldn't convey your message within 18 minutes, then there was still work to be done. Over time, there was also talk of 7 minutes or 3 minutes.

3. You were not allowed to talk about politics, religion or sell from the stage. You did not come to praise a product to the skies. It had to be about ideas worth spreading. As a result, storytelling gained ground in the talks, and the TED Talks became addictive for the audience.

These three adjustments made event organisers around the world realise that things could be done differently. Today, you will not often see a 60-minute keynote at an event anymore. Exceptionally, a speaker still gets 45 minutes, but for most, it ranges between 20 and 30 minutes. Moreover, storytelling has become a must-have, and every audience wants to be inspired.

The TED format really went viral when the best talks were made available online for the general public. It meant the international breakthrough of many experts and made many dream of speaking on a TED stage.

It soon became clear that being able to put 'TEDx Speaker' on your CV was good for your personal brand. With only a few TEDx licences in a country, it was a status symbol if you were in the lineup. Well-known and renowned experts did not mind speaking for free once if it gave them a chance at an international breakthrough.

Not only did the number of TEDx licences issued increase, but also the number of events organised. In 2014, a small country like Belgium counted no less than 32 events. A TEDx stage became a place for ambitious starting speakers.

TEDx was also a breeding ground for aspiring speaker coaches. The TEDx rules stated that each speaker had to be coached by the team with the aim of ensuring compliance with the rules. You were not expected to teach the speakers to speak better; it was a protocol function. Coaches seized the opportunity to associate their name with the TEDx brand in an attempt to strengthen their status. In the land of the blind, the one-eyed man is king.

As of 2023, I hear little about TED. Occasionally, I still meet professionals who dream aloud of standing on a TEDx stage or who report about it. At the time of writing this book, there are nine TEDx events scheduled in Belgium. For the (sold-out) annual five-day congress, you now pay $10,000 for a ticket. But a 'TED Talk' is part of the vocabulary of anyone who wants to work as a speaker. And giving one is invariably on the wishlist. And that is something I can only applaud.

PODCAST ALERT
Listen to the episodes of my podcast where I engage in conversation with both TEDx speakers and coaches.

Taking the leap

Professionals take their first steps in public speaking when they give a presentation to a client or internally to colleagues within their own company. These could be sales presentations, product presentations, or annual reports, for example. Usually, they get a taste for it when they are suddenly also asked to give a keynote at a third party event. The atmosphere is different, and so is the impact. At that moment, a keynote speaker is born, and they understand what the impact of public speaking can be.

You tell your story once in front of a room full of potential clients, and you go home with appointments in your agenda. What more could you want? After speaking on third party stages a few times, many experts want to make this a part of their business. The ROI of it is much larger than what they were used to.

However, at that point, they encounter a number of obstacles:

- professionalisation of both the keynote, the performance, and the PowerPoint is needed;
- there is a need for a system to market and position yourself as a speaker;
- there is a need for a flow where the keynote, time management, and revenue models are aligned.

This is the moment when I start working with professionals to develop a signature keynote that they can use sustainably and to work on their speaker business.

Comfortable being uncomfortable

Speaking in front of a group of people and engaging them in what you are saying is, for me, the most beautiful profession in the world. This makes sense when you look at my life path. For someone who has been performing on a stage since she was seven and still does at 50, it can only be a passion.

But it's not an easy profession and is mostly underestimated. It seems to go smoothly for some speakers, including myself. I get on stage and everything seems to happen naturally, my body feels free to move, I'm not embarrassed about anything, I talk as if I'm making it up on the spot, make jokes, interact with the audience, and if something goes wrong, I improvise. I feel like a fish in water.

But what nobody realises is that it's not hours but years of experience and practice behind it.
That days of study precede it.
That I have had to deal with blackouts multiple times.
That I've stood on a stage sick as a dog, with high fever and without a voice.
That I've cried buckets from stage fright during rehearsals.

That I've struggled through performances because the audience wasn't interested, or I was at odds with co-actors.
That I felt intimidated by colleagues, making me shy and withdrawn.
That I've received loads of criticism about my appearance, my personality, my way of acting.
That I often struggled to overcome my shyness. That I constantly felt inferior and ugly.

Stamina, self-leadership, and intrinsic motivation, along with study and training, have led to the point where little now will stop me from going on stage, doing my thing, and giving my best. Professionals dream about the successful charismatic effect that a strong speaker has but don't realise that the key is being willing to feel comfortable being uncomfortable and doing the work.

The most complete experience of who you are

I've said it before, but of all the tactics available in personal branding, speaking is the most comprehensive.

An audience cannot experience more of you than when they see you speak. Seeing and hearing someone speak in person means feeling their energy and drive. It also means being able to read body language and facial expressions, experiencing the timbre of a voice, and the intonation of spoken words.

As a speaker, it's much harder to pretend to be someone you're not than when you write, for example. Your personality comes to the surface much more quickly when speaking, and your supposed personality even more quickly. And in the latter case, you're exposed.

How often have you experienced reading someone's posts, articles, or books, finding them interesting, only to be turned off by the speaker's personality when you see them on stage? You lose trust when you feel to your very roots that something's off. Or when you realise that the drive, passion, and use of big words and rousing language ultimately come from someone who turns out to be an empty shell.

That's what makes coaching speakers such a delicate matter. My heart still skips a beat whenever I see yet another booklet or article appear in which concepts like charisma, trust, and power are reduced to a series of mechanical movements, the use of muscles, the utterance of certain words in a certain intonation. When everything becomes a step-by-step plan that you must execute in order.

Practise practise practise

Recognising and naming something is entirely different from effectively deploying it. Using your hands, adopting poses such as power poses can very quickly turn you into a puppet rather than a charismatic, strong speaker.

One reason for this is insufficient practice. "But I don't want to practise too much because then I won't be spontaneous" is a common excuse I hear. Nonsense. You're insecure and unaware of what could happen if you practised more, how you could practise more and especially better. Every strong speaker is the result of repetition, adjusting, and trying again. Consciously, unconsciously, with or without coaching, in front of an audience or at home in the kitchen.

Unfortunately, a more decisive argument is the lack of time to practise. But if you compare how many days and weeks I rehearsed for a role before hitting the road with it for months, and the mere hours in which a professional expects to become a proficient speaker, you'll understand where the expertise comes from.

If you want to become an experienced speaker, you need repeated practice. Either you organise the practice yourself, at home or with a coach, or you make sure you have speaking opportunities where you can practise in front of an audience.

The latter is precisely what stand-up comedians always do. They test and practise their new material in try-outs, often given away for free in alternative circuits. Similarly, there are networks and places for speakers that will welcome you if they don't need to pay you.

Another important reason you might come across as a puppet is if you are not congruent in thinking, speaking, feeling, and doing. When you're on stage, you wear multiple hats: you're both the director and performer, both performer and observer, both star and simple you.

Let's start with the latter:

- You are both a star and simple you. By this, I mean that you are asked to stand on that stage as a result of your expertise. The spotlight is on you, there are people who find you important and want to show you to an audience, assuming that your presentation will earn them accolades. That makes you a star. But at the same time, you are you.
- You are both performer and observer. This is a very strange feeling to experience. It feels very split. You feel yourself performing, and at the same time, it's as if you're sitting in the audience.
- You are both performer and director. While you're delivering your talk, occasionally a voice can give you directions on how to do this or that, what your next move or sentence is. Like a director directing you during the performance.

The uncomfortable, uncertain feeling many speakers have is related to balancing and dealing with these hats while speaking. And actually... it's good to have some trouble with this because it means you care about your performance and your audience. That you want to do well. Professionals who claim to have no trouble with this are either bluffing or are only concerned about themselves without any interest in the audience. Or... they are in a flow. Experiencing flow while speaking is like a runner's high or catching a wave while surfing. It's a blissful feeling, but it often doesn't last very long.

Depending on how you feel and how you've prepared, some hats might weigh more heavily, and you might become too focused on one of them, causing you to lose balance. When you are balanced, you can gently switch between the hats. Because they are there, regardless. Gently switching is what I referred to as learning to be comfortable with being uncomfortable. It's not comfortable to feel like you're watching yourself and seeing everything.

If you can switch gently, you can also be congruent in your speaking, feeling, moving. Why? Because your focus can remain on conveying a message you believe in, articulated with images, words, arguments that you also believe in, aligned with your personal values.

The one domino

Just as you create a character from the inside out, as a speaker, you also work from the inside out. You look for the intrinsic and extrinsic motivation of the character/speaker to come forward with certain information.

So, not: I memorise my bullet points by heart, and a coach tells me how to use my voice, what the best intonation is, and how I should move. But rather: What exactly do I want to convey, to whom, what result do I aim for, why, and do I stand behind what I want to say?

I discuss this with every speaker I work with. Time and again, elements come up that will make a speaker feel uncomfortable, not find their words, lose the thread, and move awkwardly. The body tells what the mind thinks and the heart feels. Solving that is the domino that will set everything in motion and ensure congruence.

Signature keynote

I work with professionals who either want to make public speaking a key pillar of their business model or for whom giving speeches is an important part of their role and status. I typically start working with them when they already have experience or have one or more keynotes or speeches scheduled. For beginners, I recommend starting with group training. Occasionally, I make exceptions when I encounter a rough diamond.

I often hear speakers complain about having to create a new keynote for each assignment at the request of the organiser. When you are serious about making public speaking a pillar of your personal branding, it's important to develop a signature keynote.

A signature keynote is your base keynote aimed at your most common target audience and addresses the most important topic within which you position yourself as an expert. Naturally, it makes sense to personalise your keynote to the theme and audience of the event you are speaking at; that is your task as a professional speaker. However, if you build your signature keynote modularly, you can replace and adjust parts depending on the variations of the theme you also want to offer, just like with LEGO. Start by offering your signature keynote. Over time, you can add another topic within your expertise and expand your offerings.

Another question that organisers might ask you as a keynote speaker and expert is: do you also have a book? And that's not so strange because a book is one of the tactics that can elevate your personal brand to the next level.

The Book – The author

Having a book published under your name is on the bucket list for many professionals. And while in the past your chance to become an author entirely depended on traditional publishers known for having stacks of manuscripts they never looked at, today, that opportunity is entirely at your initiative.

Nowadays, traditional publishers no longer have the monopoly. You can start your own publishing house (as I did for a while), you can simply have your book printed without a publisher, and there are book coaches who guide you through the writing process.

Judging by the number of titles launched monthly, it must still be a booming business for those generating revenue from the production side. But what about the author? Writing a book is a long-term and intensive process. Moreover, the possibility that you will never be compensated for the time invested in writing is real, as is temporarily losing revenue because you cannot work. Considering that the author's royalties from a book amount to 10% of the sales price (the copy that you have in your hands has earned me 3 euros), you know you're not writing to put bread on the table.

Does writing a book increase your expert status or not? I am the author of nine titles in fiction and non-fiction, published by traditional publishers. I have also been a publisher of short stories for other well-known fiction authors with a unique concept. I work with international speakers who write books, with entrepreneurs who have their books written, and with entrepreneurs who have self-published a book or want to write one.

My answer is:
YES, it can boost your expert status.
And NO, it doesn't happen just by writing (or having written) the book.
Confusing?

Writing a book is a commendable task. You invest a lot of time, energy, lonely moments, and a great deal of dedication into it – even if you work with a ghostwriter or AI. And when you finally have submitted your edited and approved manuscript to the publisher, a sigh of relief goes through you because now everything is in the publisher's hands. A few months later, cardboard boxes in your garage are winking at you, and you're plotting a book launch that will shoot your book into the market like a rocket. Let that expert status come!

A book is a (marketing) tool, an instrument that can be used to strengthen your personal branding and as a strategic tool to generate more revenue. If little is done with it after publication, if you don't build a house around it, its impact fades away after three months.

And this is something I often see happening with business books. For authors, a book can seem more like an endpoint, a finish line they've finally crossed, rather than a starting point. Whereas a book is a vehicle that can take your reader from A to B and become your customer. But you have to do quite a bit for that. You need to set the pawns for this chess game correctly. To do this well, there are several important questions you need to ask yourself. Preferably before you even start writing your book. One of them seems off topic but it is not: what kind of life do you want to lead?

A book can set you on different paths, but you have to decide which one. Do you want to live off royalties, or do you want to establish a high-quality personal brand with a business in the market, where quality also applies to your private life? Because then you can play the game in a way that yields the most results for you.

Another question you need to ask yourself in advance is: are your network and visibility large enough to launch a book? It makes no sense to do all that work aiming to increase your expert status if you're not visible elsewhere. The chance of going from zero to hero with your book is small, and while you can dream about it, you shouldn't count on it.

Is a book always a bad idea? Not at all. If the timing is right, your personal brand is on the rise, and your topic is hot, then you should definitely go for it. A book has always been the tool of the trusted expert, the personality brand, and the thought leader. But it's not the only one (although it is the most expensive).

If you also unleash the entrepreneur within, you'll see opportunities that can benefit you:

- You get invited for keynotes, put your book in the deal and generate leads.
- You get invited for keynotes more quickly and can increase your price.
- You turn your book into a fantastic marketing product.
- You can create derivative products.
- You have content written for an entire year. Yay!
- You have a chance for a small passive income.

Have you decided to write a book? Great! Now you need to find an answer to a whole series of questions.

What's your approach?

There are different formats for writing a business book. Here are some, from easiest to more difficult:

- Interview 10 experts in your industry, add a preface and a postscript.
- Ensure you're one of those interviewed in someone else's book and ask to elaborate further in a chapter.
- Write solid blog posts for a year and compile them into a book.
- Hire a ghostwriter, get interviewed for hours, and have everything written out.
- Make a combination of the above.
- Co-write a book with another expert and divide the chapters.
- Write a book from scratch entirely by yourself.

Other questions are:

Do you work with a writing coach or can you do it yourself?
In recent years, it has become possible to hire writing coaches. Writing is a lonely process. Having a sparring partner, sounding board, or fresh perspective is certainly advisable. If you're making your debut in writing, it's also wise to seek guidance on structure, style, planning, etc.

Do you want to self-publish or work with a publisher?
Both strategies have their advantages and disadvantages. A renowned publisher offers you structure and support, bears some of the costs, and has a distribution network. Moreover, as an author, you gain more credibility by collaborating and have a greater chance of visibility in the traditional press. The downside is that you may earn less from your book, cannot make all the choices yourself, you give up some of your rights, and you must be selected by them.

Is self-publishing better?
It grants you the independence to make all decisions yourself, but that's not always a blessing because you also bear the costs, and many choices need to be made. You could potentially earn more, provided you have a large network, your own market, and market value.

Self-publishing is a smart move if you are well-known in your industry. However, if that's not the case, self-publishing mainly offers the satisfaction of having a book under your name.

Which language should I write in?
The language in which you publish your book does not necessarily have to be the language in which you write. Be aware that translating a book can cost thousands of euros and add extra months before the book will be available in stores. Whether it makes sense depends on your target audience, which language your customers speak the most, and whether you work internationally or not. To enhance the impact of a book in English, you also need to consider the content carefully. For example, ensure that your examples, case studies, and data are internationally relevant.

And of course: what will my book be about?
Do you have enough material to fill at least 150 pages? Do you have a specific angle from which you will share your expertise? Do you have a clear idea of your reader? Do you have a (preliminary) clear idea about the format? How do you plan to work on the book? Will you work in a structured, systematic manner? Will you allocate a research period? Have you thought about how you want to organise your writing process?

You can devise a plan or seek guidance. I've written in various genres and tried and tested different methodologies. My main conclusion is that you will discover yourself as a writing person and that you should not let anyone dictate your way of working.

PODCAST ALERT
In my podcast, I speak with various experts who also have books to their names. You can draw inspiration from them and make your own choices.

The Podcast - host or guest?

You can stand on a stage and speak, you can stand in front of a camera and speak, or you can stand in front of a microphone and speak. Using just your voice can create magic.

When I passed the voice test of VRT, the national public service broadcaster for the Flemish community of Belgium, in 2002, I was allowed to work as a presenter for the main national radio channels. The voice test was rigorous, and I remember entering the examination room (studio) with my heart pounding. Everything had to be not just good, but perfect, according to the national broadcaster's standards. I had to speak perfect Standard Dutch, with no dialectal sounds or words, and the texts I had to write had to be well-written, attractive, and clearly articulated for the target audience of the channel. My tone of voice had to match the channel, and my voice itself had to meet the professional warmth and friendliness they wanted to associate with their channels. I was as proud as punch when I went home with my A certificate. I couldn't have coped if that hadn't been the case after years of following Dutch pronunciation lessons and having graduated as a master in performing arts.

I got to work at Klara, the VRT's classical music channel, which also turned out to be the strictest and most difficult channel to present. The radio programme I was allowed to present for several seasons was called Het Gelag. Het Gelag aired on Sunday evenings and was about the literary cafés during the 1900s. Journalist Eric Min did all the research and wrote the scripts, while music compiler Marc Van Rompaey put together the playlist of world music and jazz. Het Gelag was immediately an odd one out in the programming, just as I was among the team of presenters who knew much more about music than I did.

I fell in love with my programme, even though it was sometimes extremely difficult to get the sentences and words pronounced correctly from my mouth. The language advisor wanted each name to be pronounced in the language of origin and not an 'adapted' version of it. Specifically, this meant that sometimes I spoke three languages in one sentence. And no, not Dutch, English, and French, but for example, Spanish with Russian and a bit of Swedish thrown in. Feeling the stress yet?

Presenting this programme taught me how you can reach into someone's heart and soul by using your voice and a microphone technically and more consciously. A 'radio voice' can be developed, and if you have one, then you have a powerful tool of persuasion. Because good voices not only instil confidence, they seduce.

This is why the third tactic that can strengthen your personality brand, for me, is podcasting – apart from the trend it has also become. With podcasting, you can go in two directions: you can host your own podcast or you can focus on being a guest on podcasts. The latter is discussed in the chapter on PR. Right now, I'm talking about hosting your own podcast. Podcasting offers unique advantages over writing content for social media, especially in terms of building an audience and the influence of algorithms. I'll give you five reasons why podcasting is a more interesting tool.

Deep connection with your audience

With podcasting, you can develop a deeper, or should I say 'more intimate', connection with your audience than with written content on social media. Due to the intimacy of audio, you can convey your thoughts, emotions, and personality in a more captivating manner. Listeners can hear your tone, humour, and passion, which aids in building trust and a good rapport.

Longer attention span

Podcasts can last longer, ranging from 30 minutes to over an hour, allowing for in-depth discussions and exploration of complex topics, unlike social media posts which are often limited to a few sentences or a short video clip. This leads to a more engaged and invested audience. Podcasting enables you to showcase your authenticity and personality in ways that written content often struggles with. By hearing your voice and the natural flow of conversations, listeners can connect with your authentic self.

Authenticity and personality

This personal touch makes your brand more human and builds a stronger connection with your audience. For this reason, I often find it regrettable when podcasts are merely the extracted mp3 from a video recording of a conversation. Once a camera is pointed at you, you start to speak and behave differently, losing a bit of intimacy.

Flexibility and multitasking

Podcasts offer the advantage of flexibility and the ability to reach your audience during various activities. Unlike written content and video, which require visual attention, podcasts allow people to listen while commuting, exercising, cooking, or performing other tasks. This capability for multitasking thus increases your reach and ensures your message can be easily consumed.

Less dependence on algorithmic reach

Unlike social media platforms, where algorithms can limit the organic reach of your content, podcasts offer more independence. While social media algorithms prioritise popular or trending content, podcasts rely more on follower loyalty and word-of-mouth recommendations. Of course, you still need to ensure people hear about your podcast and you are compelled to create content on social media to find listeners.

These are the reasons why podcasting is advantageous, but there are naturally some disadvantages too. Listening to podcasts doesn't allow for easy immediate interaction with listeners. Leaving comments and starting a conversation isn't as commonplace as it is with posts. You also don't have contact details of your listeners, you don't know their names, can't check their profiles. You have to continuously motivate them to follow you on other channels.

If you have a sharp, grating or cracked voice, then podcasting may not work to your advantage. People might be turned off. You might be better off focusing on video. With video, we still hear your voice, but you can employ other means of communication with your body language, your presence, and your clothing to let people get to know you.

My love for podcasting

In the summer of 2020, as the first wave of Covid-19 conquered the world, I decided to tackle three things on my bucket list: participating in the Dodentocht (Death March), having long conversations with fascinating people, and recording a podcast that would feed my curiosity.

> **The Dodentocht** (the Death March) is an annual event where about 15,000 motivated walkers and runners of all ages complete a 100-kilometre journey through the village and the region I live in in Belgium. Launched in 1970 by the youth club in our village, it has since grown into an internationally known event. It's moving to see and experience how a village is overwhelmed by a crowd of sturdy heroes at the starting line, and to see them the next day, stumbling over the finish line as exhausted souls. Prouder than at the start because they persevered.

While my 18-year-old son participated for the first time in 2023 and got to the finish running, as one of the first 500, the traditional edition of the march is not for me, and I call myself a 'sidewalk tourist' who cheers on the walkers while drinking a cocktail. However, in 2020, due to the pandemic and the ban on gatherings, an alternative edition was organised. This time, the Dodentocht would not last 24 hours but participants would have four weeks to complete 100 kilometres, anywhere, as long as your walks were tracked by their system. I know that this might sound like a bland alternative to the true aficionados, but this was my chance. I decided to walk at least 10 x 10 kilometres, each time inviting someone to join me for a walk and a conversation. We recorded our talk, and it was posted online as Brave New Human.

The organisation asked me to become the godmother of this exceptional edition. The virologist Marc Van Ranst had accepted the role of godfather.

My guests were Peter Hinssen (Nexxworks), CEO Caroline Craenhals (Belgian Scrap Terminal), CEO Nele Van Damme (Upgrade Estate), CEO Dimitri Barbe (Make Sense), CEO Mathieu Renier (Sparkx), virologist Marc Van Ranst, philosopher Ruben Mersch, education disruptor Kristien Bruggeman, professor of clinical psychology Mattias Desmet, Former Special Forces Operator Stijn Swijns, and artist Koen Vanmechelen.

Those were fantastic weeks. Each podcast episode turned out to be two hours long. The recording was raw, sometimes with too much wind, lengthy silences, heavy breathing, cars loudly passing by. Far from perfect. I thought nobody would listen, but the opposite was true. The authenticity and rawness were refreshing for listeners. Many people listened during their own walks or runs, while working, cooking, or driving. The concept also inspired others to start walking podcasts. But it also yielded something for my guests themselves. They discovered stories and visions within themselves that they had not articulated before, and afterwards, they were also invited for other podcasts or interviews. In the summer of 2024, I picked up the title 'Brave New Human' again and pivoted it into a journey where I go deeper in the topic of how we can become brave new humans in the current era.

For this book, I produced and hosted the Own Your Story Podcast, a series of interviews on all aspects of personal branding. Check out the QR code in this book.

You don't need much to start podcasting. You can make a decent recording with a smartphone. But you can also go all the way and work with a production house, as I do when hosting podcasts for my corporate clients.

What's more important is to decide what your podcast is about, and whether you want to use a specific format. I'll give you a few ideas:

- Solo episodes versus conversations;
- Deliberately short or deliberately long episodes;
- With video or audio only;
- On location, in a studio, or simply at home;
- Do you want to create a limited series, or a podcast that will run for years?

Also, in determining the focus of your podcast, it's worth spending more than one night thinking about it. I notice there are often two directions: either very niche-oriented or very broad. Both have their advantages and disadvantages.

If the goal of your podcast is to further position yourself in the market as an expert in XYZ, then it seems logical that your podcast should cover that specific topic. Focus, niche, you probably already know this. But the question is whether you can sustain this for 100 episodes.

So do the test and come up with at least 20 episode topics you can talk about for at least 10 minutes without repeating yourself. Additionally, list at least 20 names of people you can contact to guest on your podcast. If you can do it, then your niche is rich enough, and so is your knowledge.

Opting for a niche subject means it might take longer to find the right audience and that the group might remain small. But is that a problem? As long as a small audience converts into trust and sales, there's nothing wrong with that. As long as the pond doesn't dry up.

If you go broad in your conversations, finding topics and guests will be a no-brainer. Growing an audience will be too. Think of themes like entrepreneurship and mindset. But how do you distinguish yourself in this area? With these podcasts, I often notice that the host loses positioning when both the host and guests aren't strong enough.

Although you as a host have a congenial and spontaneous conversation in mind, the pitfall is thinking that you then don't need to prepare. A good conversation stems from asking good and appropriate questions. It requires leadership from the host to steer a conversation in the right direction and to prepare thoroughly. When I guide podcasters, these are invariably the action points on the agenda.

Podcasting can seriously boost your positioning and fame, but being consistent and maintaining it is not to be underestimated. Most of us (myself included) start off overconfident with the idea of posting a podcast online weekly. But if you don't build a machine, process, system behind it to make it a part of your operation and seek help, at some point you will lose track. You might skip a week and then another, and before you know it, you find yourself apologising to your audience that it's been a month since you uploaded an episode. I plead guilty. It's happened to me too.

PR

By producing your own podcast, writing your book, and creating online content, you take the reins in building your own network and increasing your visibility. This is what we call 'owned media'. Here, you dictate what you want to say, when you want to say it, and how you want to say it.

But there's also Earned Media. This involves leveraging the audiences of others to spotlight yourself. Think about giving a keynote or being a guest on a podcast. For these occasions, you're invited to act as an expert within someone else's network. An interview in the newspaper, or being a guest on a news programme on radio or television are other examples of earned media or also public relations. In public relations, you work on your relationship with other networks. It's crucial that you're seen or heard in these contexts.

However, it's equally important not to put all your eggs in this basket. A common mistake among leaders is to communicate only when absolutely necessary, and then through earned media. While strengthening relationships is important, you must not forget that each outlet has its own agenda, policy, and philosophy into which they fit you as a guest. This can lead to frustrations when headlines of interviews are

taken out of context, or statements are distorted. Without owned media to fall back on, you risk becoming a scapegoat.

Besides owned and earned media, there's also paid media. This refers to media exposure you pay for. This includes advertisements (online and offline), sponsored posts, and all content for which you pay to reach a broader audience. A popular example is a Google AdWords campaign or sponsoring a post on Facebook to reach potential customers.

When you want to enter someone else's audience, you also need to become visible to them. That's why escaping online visibility is not an option. On the contrary, you build your owned media online, so others can get to know you before inviting you.

Finding the right stages and the right contacts can be outsourced to PR agencies or freelancers, or you can start on your own. And then, LinkedIn, Sales Navigator, and a spreadsheet are your best friends. Generally, it's best to start a year in advance. Many events take place annually. You can start building a relationship before you need anything from them.

Summary of Chapter 15: The tactics in Real Life personality branding

16 things to remember:

1. Online personal branding is the biggest dimension but not the oldest.
2. In real life, personal branding was the only branding we knew before the rise of social media platforms.
3. In real life, personal branding is still important in corporate life.
4. When you start your personal branding process online and you get invited for real life appearances like keynotes, podcasts etcetera, then that is a sign of status.
5. Becoming a speaker is offering your audience the most complete experience of you.
6. As a speaker, you need to learn to be comfortable being uncomfortable.
7. Becoming a good keynote speaker demands dedication and practice.
8. Creating a signature keynote is key for a speaker.
9. Writing a book or being the author of a book equals more status, more opportunities.
10. Learn to leverage the opportunities and be proactive in promoting your book.
11. Everyone can be an author, but not everyone is a writer.
12. Being a guest in a podcast is smarter than hosting your own podcast.
13. Free yourself from algorithm slavery by producing a podcast.
14. Know how to leverage owned media, paid media and earned media.
15. Earned media is harder to get, speed is important and so is building a relationship with the press.
16. Don't forget to add PR in your branding process.

Chapter 16: What about the ROI?

And the ROI, ianka. The ROI... measurement is knowledge, right?

But how do you measure the 'return on your investment', the result of all your efforts to grow your personal brand? Many people don't see the importance of personal branding, simply because it's not always easy to see a direct ROI in terms of sales or revenue. After all, there's no perfectly precise formula for measuring the ROI of your personal branding. But that doesn't mean it can't be measured at all. In my experience, to measure ROI, you need to look at personal branding from two perspectives: short-term and long-term, with the latter being the most important.

During one of my one-day boot camps on personal branding, a participant confidently shared that they had experimented with different content formats for a month, ranging from text and video to carousels, etc., and measured each for its ROI. Their principle was not to spend time and effort on something that leads to nothing. While I completely understand their reasoning, my surprised face could not have gone unnoticed. In a month, you can't measure enough to make decisions. Too many different parameters and too short a period. Anyway, it takes much longer than you might think to become immersed in your personal branding strategy. There can be a long journey between being, wanting, and doing. And once you've got it down, it still takes months, or even longer before you can really measure the significant results.

However, it's understandable that as you begin to profile yourself as a leader within your niche, your name recognition grows, and you attract followers, you'll want to be able to measure your impact. You can start by tracking the following short-term ROI markers for personal branding.

1. **Reach**
   A good starting point is to track the size and growth of your followers across various online platforms. If your goal is to be recognised as an expert in your niche, a strong online following is necessary to lend legitimacy to your personal brand. Keep an eye on the analytics.

2. **Engagement**
   Anyone can click 'follow' on someone's profile, so how do you know if they're genuinely paying attention to your posts? That's why engagement is such an important metric. By monitoring the insights and engagement of your social media posts and looking at factors like likes, comments, and views, you get an idea of your audience's connection with you. However, the only real engagement that matters most to you as an entrepreneur is, of course, when someone from the crowd stands up and wants to start a conversation with you in the hope of becoming your client, investor, or employee.

3. **Website traffic**
   Your website is a fantastic place to direct your social media traffic. Using Google Analytics tools, you can measure and analyse direct and referral traffic to your website. Pay attention to which pages people visit and how long they stay on each page.

4. **Press analysis**
   As your personal brand grows, you want more and more people to know your name and talk about you. One way to measure this is by analysing your press releases in traditional and online media. But also, requests for keynotes and guest appearances on podcasts are a significant indicator.

While all these are useful metrics to get an idea of the success of your personal brand, some are also debatable in importance. For instance, you have no idea about the group of people who faithfully follow you but don't leave comments or likes. Yet this group could produce your best customers. You might have thousands of followers who like everything you do but would never buy anything from you. What then is the value of these numbers? That's why I believe the most valuable ROI can be seen in the long-term benefits that can be identified by the following markers:

Fulfilment

Fulfilment is defined as the profound joy and happiness that comes from living in alignment with who you are.

Flow

Being in flow, also known as being in the zone, is defined as a state of being where you are fully immersed in the activity you are doing. The things you can create and accomplish in this state are incredible. If your personal brand is too demanding and too ambitious, you won't experience flow but continuous stress.

Becoming a leader

In my opinion, one of the most important ROIs in personal branding is becoming a leader. Having a positive impact on the world, leading and inspiring a group of people. It's so fulfilling to receive messages from people saying that I inspired them to become better.

Creating opportunities

When you're known as an expert and a leader in your niche, the opportunities you get are incredible; often, they come from unexpected places. You get the chance to write for renowned magazines, opportunities to speak at places you've never heard of, to meet people on your bucket list, to attend special events.

Future-proofing yourself!

Your job, your business — whether you own it or work there — will likely not be the only thing you do forever. Once you leave, you leave that brand and/or that company behind, and wherever you go next, you have to start over. But your personal brand is always with you and can be taken anywhere, even if you change direction.

It should be clear by now that I am not someone who measures growth against numbers or data but against meaning, value, and fulfilment. I hope you are like that too. Because then, by now, you should realise that in personal branding, everything revolves around the personality undergoing the process.

Summary of Chapter 16: What about the ROI?

3 things to remember:

1. Sorry, but personal branding is a long-term strategy.
2. You don't easily see the return on investment in data.
3. But keep an eye on: engagement, website traffic, reach, leads, opportunities, relationship building.

PART 6: OWN YOUR ARTIFICIAL IDENTITY

Earlier in this book, I indicated that personal branding has three dimensions. The first and most deployed is online personal branding with platforms like LinkedIn, X, Instagram and TikTok that determine your impact through their algorithms. Then you have the second dimension where everything happens In Real Life, dealing with physical presence and products. The third dimension is that of virtual personal branding.

When I wrote the first edition of this book, the edition now available in Dutch, my native tongue, I took a first step to give a point of view about that third yet unknown dimension. With this translation, I have taken the opportunity to make it an updated edition. It is barely a year later but for this chapter it was certainly necessary. And if you are reading this chapter in 2026, then please take the year of publication into account.

Chapter 17: Welcome to the Metaverse: a new digital frontier

Let's kick things off with a term that's been buzzing around the tech and business world over the last few years: the Metaverse. If you're imagining a dystopian sci-fi world, you're not entirely off, but the reality might be more exciting.

As Matthew Ball writes in *The Metaverse: And How It Will Revolutionize Everything*, the Metaverse is defined as "a massively scaled and interoperable network of real-time rendered 3D virtual worlds which can be experienced synchronously and persistently by an effectively unlimited number of users with an individual sense of presence". Essentially, it's a vast digital universe where you can live, work, play, and interact with others just like in the physical world. Think about it as you walk around as yourself in a video game, doing stuff, interacting with people, living a Second Life (remember the game?).

Sure, it's going to take a few more years for the Metaverse to fully materialise. But that hasn't stopped companies from diving headfirst into experimentation. From virtual reality concerts to digital real estate, brands are already carving out their territories in this new world. Nike was one of the first major brands to develop their own immersive world. According to Roblox, 'Nikeland' received over 31.5 million visits in 2023, indicating that the brand has been massively successful with its metaverse entry strategy. These aren't just gimmicks – they're strategic moves to establish brand presence and engage with tech-savvy audiences in innovative ways.

Brands leading the charge in the Metaverse

So, why are big brands so eager to invest in the Metaverse? It's simple: the potential for engagement is enormous. Imagine attending a virtual fashion show where you can buy digital clothes for your avatar or visiting a virtual dealership to test drive a car in a stunning 3D environment. The Metaverse allows brands to create immersive, interactive experiences that go beyond traditional advertising. It's a playground for creativity, enabling companies to build deeper connections with their audiences and make more money.

Take the fashion industry, for instance. In 2021, Balenciaga collaborated with Fortnite to create exclusive digital outfits, blending high fashion with gaming culture. Similarly, Coca-Cola has auctioned off its first NFT (non-fungible token), which includes a virtual wearable jacket. These ventures were not just about novelty; they're about staying relevant and engaging with younger, digital-native generations on platforms they love.

The Metaverse and personality branding

Now, let's draw a parallel to personality branding. Just as companies are investing in their virtual presence, individuals can also leverage the Metaverse to enhance their personal brands. Imagine attending virtual networking events, hosting webinars in a fully immersive environment, or even creating a digital twin that can interact with others on your behalf.

Pioneers of Virtual Personality Branding

Several forward-thinking individuals have already started building their personal brands in the Metaverse, reaping the benefits of being early adopters. One of them is Cathy Hackl, often referred to as the "Godmother of the Metaverse."

> ***"The world's next Coco Chanel is probably a 10-year-old girl currently designing avatar skins in Roblox."***
>
> – Cathy Hackl

Hackl is a futurist and tech executive who advises companies on how to navigate and leverage the Metaverse. She has established a strong personal brand by sharing insights, speaking at conferences, and engaging with a growing online community interested in the future of digital worlds. Her presence in the Metaverse has allowed her to extend her influence, attract new business opportunities, and establish herself as a thought leader in this emerging field.

One of the most famous examples is Paris Hilton. Known for her glamorous 'pink' branding in the physical world, Hilton has expanded her empire into the Metaverse. She hosts virtual events and parties, creating immersive experiences for her fans. She's also ventured into selling digital wearables and NFTs, blending her fashion sense with cutting-edge technology. By doing so, Hilton not only stays relevant but also opens up new revenue streams and maintains her status as a trendsetter.

The same goes for Snoop Dogg. Like Paris Hilton, Snoop Dogg doesn't just talk about the Metaverse, he also hosts events in the Metaverse, films videos in the Metaverse, and makes games in the Metaverse.

The Oscar-winning actress and Hello Sunshine founder Rees Witherspoon once tweeted:

"In the (near) future, every person will have a parallel digital identity. Avatars, crypto wallets, digital goods will be the norm. Are you planning for this?"

As long as the Metaverse looks like a video game and you have the appearance of a lego puppet, I'm not very interested in joining. At this point, the concept reminds me a bit of the movie *Walle-e* (2008), where people escaped the real and lost planet earth for a virtual life. But watching the podcast interview between Lex Fridman and Mark Zuckerberg gave us a glimpse of what could become a 'reality'. Conducted entirely in a virtual environment, this interview showcased the incredible realism and immersive experience possible in the Metaverse. Fridman and Zuckerberg's avatars were able to interact in a lifelike manner, they looked themselves, making it almost indistinguishable from a face-to-face conversation. That conversation showed us the potential of the Metaverse to revolutionise personal interactions, providing a glimpse into a future where geography no longer limits our ability to connect.

So, why shouldn't you start exploring what the Metaverse has to offer for your personal brand: new collaborations, global reach, innovation and creativity, enhanced engagement, and future-proofing your brand? In the end, whether you're a brand or an individual, the Metaverse represents a new dimension for storytelling, engagement, and interaction.

Let's say building your personal brand in the Metaverse is a long-term goal. How do we get there? Or better, how are the companies behind this innovation preparing us for this next dimension, where our physical identity becomes irrelevant and only our brain power is needed to drive a new dimension economy?

My answer is: generative AI.

Seeding the Artificial Identity

On November 30, 2022, a digital bomb exploded on the internet. That's when ChatGPT was launched. For many people, this date marks a new milestone in their lives. Quotes like these circulated on social media:

1. AI will not take your job, someone using AI will.
2. Master AI before it masters you.
3. To replace XYZ, clients will need to accurately describe what they want. We are safe, people.

From *Oppenheimer* director Chris Nolan and Harari, we have also incorporated the phrase "AI's Oppenheimer moment" into our vocabulary. There are clearly two camps: those who are cautious, ringing the alarm bell, insisting on immediate and comprehensive ethical rules for Big Tech, and those who behave as if they can raid the candy store. I'll leave out the group that thinks AI should be banned entirely. They are too late. AI has already been around for a long time and is here to stay.

Generative AI is capable of turning text into speech, image, video and the list will go on. Gone are the days of endlessly writing bad mails or breaking your head over a social media post. ChatGPT will fix it.

What was bad disappears. What was very good becomes mediocre. What was good, too. The new genius has yet to be revealed. And that new genius will be created by language. Not by a paintbrush, not by a camera, not by clay. But by giving a command in language to an artificial intelligence that will then create something that will hopefully amaze you.

For the masses, the world's largest amusement park has opened, where everyone can enjoy all the attractions for free. Generative AI is like kindergarten, where we are playfully accustomed to a new way of thinking, creating, doing, and communicating. We create an avatar profile photo, a DALL-E generated superwoman representation of yourself, or your custom GPT that answers questions on your behalf, or we train an AI that writes texts in our tone of voice. Most users of GenAI, deepfake, and voice cloning primarily see the entertainment value and the productivity hack that gives you more free time and money. I see it as a playful way to become accustomed to deploying a virtual and more artificial version of ourselves.

Summary of Chapter 17: Welcome to the Metaverse

6 things to remember:

1. She's not really there yet, but the seeds are already being planted.
2. The big brands are already buying in, the first personal brands too.
3. While the Metaverse still feels unreal, GenAI is there to pave the way and prepare us for it.
4. We are all playing in the AI kindergarten, while being observed.
5. From now on, we won't read or write poorly written texts anymore, but we will read poorly prompted AI results.
6. The new genius in art and literature must be rediscovered.

Chapter 18: The messy middle

"As far as AI is concerned, we're in the messy middle, between opportunity and threat," said Randi Zuckerberg, CEO at Zuckerberg Media during the WOW conference in Bruges in 2024.

The messy middle that I want to delve deeper into in this book is one that the average citizen doesn't concern themselves with: identity fraud in the creation of AI doppelgängers and voice cloning without consent.

The biggest threat: identity fraud

This problem is currently mainly affecting famous artists, politicians, and personalities. This is precisely why it doesn't interest the masses – they themselves enjoy (mis)using such figures in memes, etc. You often hear them say, "It comes with the territory". But what about the musicians that discover their voice and music is being used to create new AI-generated music? What about companies that start using AI replicas of celebrities and personal brands for ad campaigns without their consent. "Bad publicity is still publicity, and we can afford such a lawsuit," they seem to think.

When I wrote the Dutch edition of this book, in the summer of 2023, the largest protest action in Hollywood history was happening.

For the first time in Hollywood film history, the unions of both writers and actors took to the streets with the same protest slogans. Both guilds are grappling with the ethical dilemmas posed by the use of AI replicas of artists that can be used 'for the rest of eternity'.

At the same time, MIT Technology Review reports, companies like Meta and Realeyes were hiring actors to make avatars more human and train their AI for as little as $300 in a three-year period.

It seems like a plot from the Netflix series *Black Mirror* or the 2013 film *The Congress*. Director-screenwriter Ari Folman addressed the issues of actors losing control over their images, the specific problems of contract negotiations over the use of AI, and the ripple effect of AI duplicating real people.

The fear most people have today is losing their jobs to AI. What I'm talking about here goes beyond losing a job. It's about losing your identity to others, to technology, which then goes on to commercialise it. A significant amount of personal data is necessary to create digital clones, which raises numerous privacy concerns due to the risk of compromising or misusing sensitive information.

Should you own your AI? Before someone else will?
How do you handle that?
In the television and film contracts I used to sign, I always had to give permission for many things unrelated to my acting work. For example, I had to agree to what they could do with the filmed material both in the post-production and distribution phases. On one hand, it sounded logical, but on the other, there was that second part of the contract article referring to 'existing and non-existing technology distribution platforms'. You got paid rights for one but not for the other. And because you couldn't imagine what all might come onto the market, you signed. I refer once more to the TV series *Kulderzipken*, from 1995. Back then, there was barely any talk of reruns, choices were selective on what could come out on video, and the nascent internet was not even considered a possibility. Now the series has been rerun for 30 years, a video of it was released, fragments are available on the internet, and you can watch the series on various streaming channels. There's often mention of a third season. Who says they won't just artificially create

my character with my likeness without consulting me, should there be any commercial success attached to it for the broadcaster?

Who gives permission to bring a deceased person back to life through AI and commercialise it? If there's a Michael Jackson AI Döppelganger, and 'new' music from him is released? What's the value of that? And to whom does the copyright belong?

Less than a year later, you can make a list of lawsuits alleging unlawful use of the voice and likeness of artists, who are not always deceased.

In March 2024, Sam Altman, CEO of OpenAI holds back the public release of its Voice Engine that can clone someone's voice in 15 seconds due to safety concerns.

> "We recognize that producing language that resembles people's voices poses serious risks that are particularly salient in an election year. We work with U.S. and international partners in government, media, entertainment, education, civil society and beyond to ensure we incorporate their feedback in development," OpenAI said.
>
> On their blog we read: "We believe that any widespread use of synthetic speech technology should be accompanied by voice authentication experiences that verify that the original speaker is knowingly adding their voice to the service and a no-go voice list that detects and prevents the creation of voices that are too similar to prominent figures.

Two months later, OpenAI was forced to apologise to actor Scarlett Johansson for using her voice (or at least a voice that sounded very much like hers) on its latest chatbot after she refused a collaboration.

Who will be setting the rules: authorities or companies?

Authorities are slowly setting up regulations. From June 2024, the use of artificial intelligence in the EU will be regulated by the AI Act, the world's first comprehensive AI law.

In the US, several individual states are reviewing laws or proposing new legislation that would criminalise synthetic media that deals with the making or sharing of non-consensual deepfakes. But it is going too slowly.

Since I first saw DeepTomCruise in 2021, I spoke with several AI developers about developing your own AI replica watermark. This encompasses not only your intellectual property but also your name, your tone of voice, your language usage, your voice, your image, likeness, your body language, your movement.

It felt like I was talking to the moon. The most common rejection I heard was "It's too complicated, why should we?" Two years later, a positive answer came from the creators of DeepFakeCruise themselves: Metaphysic.

Metaphysic already was the industry leader in generative AI and machine learning, creating photo-realistic high-quality content but combined with an ethics-first approach. With their product Metaphysic Pro, they could effectively help actors to use generative artificial intelligence algorithms to create their own face, voice and performance data over time, as well as help 'manage' how it is used by third parties, including consent, compensation and the thorny issue of copyright, which is still being examined in courts.

Metaphysic co-founder and CEO Thomas Graham said in a statement, "AI will change content creation and storytelling forever. Whether you are an actor, performer, sportsperson or just a concerned citizen, it is critical that everyone takes active steps to protect their personal data that can be used to create a perfect AI version of your likeness or performance.

"We need to support a secure, transparent platform for performers, IP holders and filmmakers to coordinate the use of personal data to create AI content. And it needs to have consent and compensation at its heart."

Metaphysic unveiled a strategic partnership with CAA, the talent agency that represents stars like Tom Hanks, Paris Hilton and Anne Hathaway. CAA had decided not to wait for the law to catch up, but to make lawsuits easier when there is an infringement of their rights.

Threats but also opportunities

It may seem like I am entirely against AI replicas, but the opposite is true. What I am against is making the creation of your AI replica the business of your employer, allowing them to make the decisions. Your AI replica is a part of your artificial identity. It belongs to you.

The possibilities for the film industry are immense. With an AI replica, you can go much further in storytelling and execution. For now, I don't think cost savings are the issue, especially with the rights that will be paid to the artists themselves.

But thanks to AI replicas, you can make actors look younger or older where makeup falls short, film dangerous scenes more easily, and fix mistakes in post-production, to name a few. These adjustments do not have to be to the detriment of the actor. With your own AI replica and a good deal, you might actually be better off.

That evolution of implementing visual effects combined with AI has been going on for years in the VFX industry. Being married to a VFX compositor and supervisor for national and international movies, I witnessed the change in the industry years ago. While it is still hard work and not an easy fix as many people think it is, the results are astonishing.

Robert Zemeckis, the director of my all-time favourite movie *Back to the Future*, starring Michael J. Fox, started filming the motion picture *Here* in January 2023.

This film adaption of the graphic novel *Here* chronicles the lives of several families connected by a unique place they all inhabit. Spanning generations, it captures the essence of the human experience in its truest form. It's a story of love, loss, laughter, and life, all unfolding right here.

The film uses a new generative artificial intelligence technology called Metaphysic Live and yes, once more this is a product created by Metaphysic. The technology creates high-resolution photorealistic face-swap and de-ageing of the actors in real time as they perform instead of using additional post-production processing methods. We see the now 66-year-old Tom Hanks de-ageing and becoming a teenager once more.

Hanks loves the technology that offers him a new way of selling his 'core product': Tom Hanks.

Deepfake detection and Blockchain

Is growing a portfolio of high-quality data assets to create your AI face, voice and performance enough to license it safely with trusted partners?

Will it protect you from infringement?

No, you have created a product that you can now 'rent out' or license. But you also need to prove it is yours and you also need to be able to detect when there is a misuse or infringement.

According to Metaphysic, you need to copyright your AI likeness, make sure the datasets are encrypted, use access restriction, key management and 2-factor authentication.

Owning your dataset is a first step in getting control of your artificial identity.

The next step is to 'watermark' it. Unfortunately, there is not yet one universal standard in 'AI' watermarking that also is designed to be a part of a cryptographic protocol. And that is necessary to detect non-consensual deepfakes.

That's why I see blockchain playing a role in the authorisation, monetisation, and tracking process of an artificial identity.

Blockchain can be used to establish and manage ownership of digital content. It creates a transparent and traceable record so it becomes easier to track the origins of media and identify instances where unauthorised alterations may have occurred. Implementing smart contracts, self-executing contracts with the terms of agreement directly written into code, so you can verify the source of content via an invisible watermark. Blockchain also allows for accurate time stamping of data, so why not timestamp the end of the contract?

I know the technology is not there yet at its fullest, but I believe it creates the new IP in the WEB3 environment.

Summary of Chapter 18: The messy middle

7 things to remember:

1. The biggest threat in GenAI is identity fraud, when your likeness is used without your consent.
2. A significant amount of personal data is necessary to create digital clones.
3. Who is the rightful owner of an AI deepfake or AI voice clone?
4. Authorities realise rules are necessary but are slow in creating them. Yet the first laws have been implemented.
5. Companies like Metaphysic take action first, because they know AI and have more skills than authorities.
6. There are threats to be considered, but also huge opportunities when ethics are well managed.
7. Can Blockchain become an important player? I think so.

Chapter 19: AI replicas for personal brands

While the A-listers in Hollywood pave the way for us, we also need to consider what an AI replica can mean for you as a professional building a personal brand. What are the pitfalls and benefits?

The use of deepfake, voice cloning, and Generative AI technologies bring both opportunities and threats to personal brands. Let's start with the threats:

- **Identity theft:** Deepfake and voice cloning technologies can be used to create realistic forgeries of a person's likeness and voice, leading to potential identity theft and unauthorised use of one's personal brand.
- **Misinformation:** These technologies can spread misinformation, creating fake videos or audio recordings that could damage reputations and mislead audiences.
- **Plagiarism and copyright infringement:** Unauthorised use of someone's voice or likeness can result in intellectual property violations, as seen in the case of Scarlett Johansson's lawsuit against OpenAI.

Despite these significant threats, there are also considerable advantages:

Productivity

One significant advantage of using GenAI and other AI tools is the improvement in productivity. Of course, we need to undergo a learning curve to use a tool effectively, and here I refer to the chapter on GIGO (Garbage In, Garbage Out). Another point of attention is not being overwhelmed by all the different software on the market that promises you heaven on earth.

By using AI to streamline your processes and reduce daily repetitive (boring) tasks, you can gain considerable time to focus on more important tasks.

You can outsource various tasks to AI and GenAI: writing emails, automating processes, generating social media posts, creating marketing materials, editing your podcast recordings, and creating snippets. And when you combine prompt writing with a custom generative pre-trained transformer model, you can ensure that you don't have to input a prompt repeatedly. More and more is becoming possible, and it's a matter of finding the tool that best suits your needs.

Scalability

For anyone who markets themselves as a product (such as solo entrepreneurs, experts, coaches) and for whom personal branding is a good strategy, AI and GenAI offer a solution to a problem: scalability.

With the advent of social media, the platform to work on your visibility has expanded. The rise of online businesses has allowed for trainings, courses, and coaching sessions to be conducted online through pre-recorded videos sold as online courses.

Although this has already enabled growth for many, GenAI and AI tools can take it a step further.

By training an AI to understand who you are, your knowledge, language use, vision, and everything that makes you unique, you can ensure that you no longer need to make videos or interact to answer questions.

Your AI replica can do the work. Your AI twin can give webinars, hold Q&A sessions, and provide personalised 1:1 coaching sessions simultaneously in various settings for a large audience.

The startups that have jumped on this new business model are popping up like mushrooms. Gradually, we are also seeing the first results: influencers creating AI versions of themselves, thought leaders, and experts passing on their books, training, and knowledge through custom GPTs that people can ask questions to, either for free or for a fee.

Slowly, you also see talking avatars appearing. As of summer 2024, the avatars look rather wooden, like a game character that vaguely resembles you, albeit 10 years younger. The voice sounds somewhat like yours, but the intonation is not quite right. It still sounds artificial and monotonous. At this point, it mostly seems like an experiment by professionals who have the time and money to invest and want to be seen as early adopters.

Training such an AI requires more work than you might think because you have to be very deliberate about your knowledge, personality, approach, and communication style. Most people are not aware of this. You need to upload all your content, ranging from blog posts, articles, books, videos, and podcasts to tweets – everything that makes you, you. And again, GIGO (Garbage In, Garbage Out) applies here.

When you decide to develop your own AI clone and choose a platform for this, there are three important questions you need to ask yourself.

The first is: Do I own the data?

The second question is: Do I want the AI of the platform to be able to use my dataset for others?

Third question: If I am no longer satisfied, can I reuse the work I have invested in on another platform? Can my AI clone 'move'?

These questions will drastically limit the choice of platform. And yet they are important. Perhaps you don't see your work as groundbreaking right now, but will that still be the case in 10 years? Who knows, you might have achieved worldwide fame by then. I certainly wish that for you if it is your ambition.

Platforms are popping up like mushrooms, but they don't all stay standing equally easily. Developments are happening so fast that a lot of capital is needed to keep investing. Especially the middlemen are the quickest to fall out. They often base their USP on features that can be quickly adopted by the tech giants.

What about customer perception and reputation?

I fully understand the appeal of an Artificial Identity, as the benefits are exactly what every entrepreneur seeks: more time, more money. Working smarter, not harder. But does it persuade potential customers to open their wallets?

In my view, there is still a long way to go. The reception of AI clones by the audience is mixed. Some customers might appreciate the innovative and scalable solutions, finding the AI interactions convenient and efficient. However, at this point, most people may hesitate to work with an AI coach because it is not authentic and lacks a 'real' personal touch. This could impact the reputation of a brand, as clients might feel that the AI lacks the genuine human connection and empathy that they value in personal interactions.

Additionally, pricing might become an issue as well. Since AI-driven services can be offered at a lower cost than in-person coaching, clients may expect reduced fees, potentially undervaluing the expertise and effort invested in creating and maintaining the AI. But I think the overall value of the knowledge will decrease too, because the 'live' impact of the personality of the expert, the charisma, the style will be lost. Balancing the benefits of scalability and productivity with maintaining trust and perceived value will be crucial for personal brands leveraging AI technologies.

Guidelines for creating an Artificial Identity

While we are now at the point of discovering what an AI clone can do for us, we ultimately need to figure out how to shape our Artificial Identity into something we want.

There are two major guidelines:

The first is congruency. Your Artificial Identity needs to align with how you present yourself online and in real life. Working on congruency in the four criteria of your personality is important: Substance, conviction, unfair advantage, and style. The more users can resonate with your AI clone because they recognise you, the better.

The second is to make your Artificial Identity part of your narrative and not just a tool. As a tool, it will only benefit your productivity but not grow your brand (and business). As part of your narrative it – for example – can become an alter ego, a persona that you've created but that aligns with your personal brand.

We are standing at the beginning of a very interesting evolution; it both frightens and excites me. How do you feel about it?

Summary of Chapter 19:
AI replicas for personal brands

7 things to remember:

1. A personal brand in business has the same threats as a Hollywood star: identity theft, misinformation and plagiarism and copyright infringement.
2. Increased productivity is one of the major advantages of AI/GenAI implementation.
3. A personal brand can finally scale with the use of GenAI: enter the AI lookalike that takes over coaching, Q&As etc.
4. What about customer perception? Will customers like dealing with an AI replica? Will they pay for it?
5. What about your reputation? Will an AI replica enhance your reputation after the gimmick is over?
6. When you start working on your artificial identity think about staying congruent with your personal brand online and in real life.
7. Don't forget to integrate your artificial identity in your narrative. Don't just use it as a tool. Be creative.

EPILOGUE: WHAT'S YOUR BRANDED COCKTAIL?

With a slightly envious gaze, I watch the cocktails being served to my family on one of our precious family weekends. I admire them as each one is a gem to behold. Just before, I had watched the bartender as he meticulously crafted each cocktail. I witnessed a choreography of carefully executed movements that were well-rehearsed. The bartender revelled in each masterpiece he completed.

There are thousands of cocktails on the market, 77 of which are recognised by the IBA, the International Bartender Association, which has been around for 50 years. Some cocktails are created based on Myers-Briggs personalities, and others are created for special occasions. It made me think of perfumes tailored to match your skin's acidity and character. Cocktails and perfumes result from research, experimentation, personalisation, and presentation. As a storyteller, I can link these four phases to personal branding.

How do you impart a strategy when you want to convey that you don't believe in a one-size-fits-all plan? It's more of a game of elements than a set plan. You first need to find the beginning and realise that everyone's beginning is different.

The work doesn't lie in what the bartender shows but in the work of the cocktail's creator. You first need to ask yourself which ingredients make a magical blend.

That it's a journey. Your journey.

In my career and entrepreneurship, I work with experts who have a personal brand or are thought leaders. They are respected and recognised by their peers, surrounded by people who support them, and have built careers that their colleagues and competitors envy. Their personal branding journey fits outside conventional paths. Although they hold different positions in various sectors and at different levels, they all share these common traits:

They are purpose-driven, fuelled by strong intrinsic motivation.
They know why they do what they do. Most people focus on what they do and how they do it. Strong personal brands do both. British-American author, motivational speaker, and organisational consultant Simon Sinek says, "Because a true sense of purpose is deeply emotional, it serves as a compass to guide us to act in ways that are fully consistent with our values and beliefs."

They exhibit self-leadership.
We are inspired by and drawn to people comfortable in their own skin. They exude balance and a strong sense of self-worth, which creates trust. Trust often stems from the willingness to be who they are without excuse or apology. When they speak, we are ready to listen and inclined to believe exactly what they say.

They do not wear blinders; on the contrary, they look beyond.
They think beyond their role and aim to influence other industries, domains, businesses, or sectors. They use new technologies and methods for this. They are respected for their expertise and viewpoint and are engaged and committed.

They are generous.
There will always be egocentric personal brands, no doubt. Still, it's noticeable that personal branding is not a Me, Myself, and I story for those who do it well. They are often generous with praise – regularly acknowledging others for their insights and contributions, both online and in person. They share information, content, and advice freely. They live in a world of abundance and are willing to invest time and energy in supporting others.

They are lifelong learners.
They know that if they are not learning and growing, they are not just standing still but falling behind. Their curiosity compels them to try new things. They seize every opportunity to learn through daily, on-the-job activities and more formal talent development programmes.

They are ambitious.
While they do more than what is expected of them today, they are focused on the future. They are always aware of or contemplating the next step. Personal branding is based on personality, but it has an aspirational element. You must be who you are while positioning yourself for the future. Personal brands show that they are not only competent where they are but also ready and eager for their next big thing.

They are curious.
They are as interested as they are interesting. Their curiosity helps them build stronger, more authentic relationships with others. It keeps them fresh by always discovering and learning more about things.

No two personal brands are the same, but I recognise similar attitudes in all of them.

Time to go

It's time to wrap up.

Why not end with my 10 commandments for personality brands?

1. A company brand is made by design. A personal brand, through a person's development.
2. It's about you, but not just about you.
3. You're in this for the long run.
4. Tools and platforms need to serve you, not the other way around.
5. A personality brand grows with your personality.
6. Creating a legacy is more rewarding than building fame.
7. Own your name.
8. Own your journey.
9. Own your AI.
10. Own your story. Or someone else will.

I will likely want to add things at the launch in a few months, because I will probably be further along in my thought process, and want to adjust some points. That's the nature of writing a book. That's why I'm producing the podcast alongside it. It's a living document where you can hear other voices as well. Use them together; it will enrich your reading experience.

This book is a book on personal branding.
But to be honest, even more it is a book on how we humans of a modern society exploit our public identity.

How we outgrow who we are and become an online persona, a personality in real life and an artificial identity in a virtual world.

Etienne Vermeersch, the philosopher-ethicist-sceptic whom I once had the privilege of interviewing for my book programme, said the following words in the Flemish newspaper *De Morgen* in 2009:

> ***"I do not claim that my insight is always the right one, but it is the result of honest research. I accept that others may come to a different conclusion, but I hope then that they too have done their homework."***

And on another occasion: "Do not believe me, think for yourself."

I can't give you better advice. I wish you a pleasant journey. Thank you for reading me.

- ianka

Do not believe me,
think for yourself

About the author

Master storyteller, multidisciplinary creator, and entrepreneur are what define ianka. Throughout her successful career as an actress in television, film, and theatre, she created opportunities to become an author, director, and producer of her own programmes on national TV and radio channels. She is a highly sought-after moderator for high-end conferences on marketing, entrepreneurship, innovation, and a speaker on personality branding and storytelling.

Personal website:

- www.iankafleerackers.com

Follow ianka on these channels

- www.linkedin.com/in/iankafleerackers
- x.com/iankafleeracker
- www.youtube.com/c/iankafleerackers

Website book:

- www.ownyourstory.be

Company:

- www.thoughtleaders.academy

Through the Thought Leaders Academy and Own Your Story Agency, ianka and her team guide entrepreneurs, experts, and C-suite executives in developing a personality brand. Leveraging her broad and in-depth professional expertise and a network of partners, they can support you in the following aspects of personal branding:

- Personal branding strategy
- Keynote development
- Online content writing

- Storytelling
- PR
- Podcasting
- Public speaking
- Business development
- LinkedIn content writing
- Book writing

Their services can take various forms:

1. Coaching, training, mentoring
2. Done-with-you: co-creation and design
3. Done-for-you: execution and management

If you're ready to start and want to know how they can support you, please fill out the contact form on iankafleerackers.com

Start Your Journey Now!

With the purchase of this book, additional online resources are available to assist you in your personal branding journey.

Book: www.ownyourstory.be

Download the workbook using this QR code or visit ownyourstory.be. Sign up and use the code **oys-now** to access the materials.

Bibliography

Part 1: Dare to get attention

- https://www.psychologiemagazine.nl/artikel/hierom-schrik-je-vaak-als-je-een-foto-van-jezelf-ziet
- https://www.wiwi.europa-uni.de/de/lehrstuhl/fine/mikro/bilder_und_pdf-dateien/WS0910/VLBehEconomics/Ausarbeitungen/MereExposure.pdf
- http://psychology.iresearchnet.com/social-psychology/social-psychology-theories/self-verification-theory/
- https://www.researchgate.net/publication/306031974_The_Looking_Glass_Lens_Self-concept_Changes_Due_to_Social_Media_Practices
- https://lesley.edu/article/perception-is-reality-the-looking-glass-self
- https://www2.deloitte.com/global/en/pages/governance-risk-and-compliance/articles/reputation-at-risk.html
- 'The Cyber effect' – Mary Aiken
- Misleading First Impressions: Different for Different Facial Images of the Same Person. Authors: Alexander Todorov and Jenny M. Porter https://journals.sagepub.com/doi/10.1177/0956797614532474
- https://www.theladders.com/career-advice/this-study-just-blew-up-a-major-myth-about-first-impressions
- https://journals.sagepub.com/doi/10.1177/00187267211002905
- https://en.wikipedia.org/wiki/First_impression_(psychology)
- Big Leap - Gay Hendricks
- https://gdpr.eu/right-to-be-forgotten/
- https://support.google.com/legal/answer/10769224?hl=en
- https://transparencyreport.google.com/eu-privacy/overview?hl=en
- Film Iedereen Beroemd - director Dominique Deruddere https://www.imdb.com/title/tt0209037/
- https://www.fastcompany.com/28905/brand-called-you
- https://tompeters.com/
- https://www.entrepreneur.com/starting-a-business/22-statistics-that-prove-the-value-of-personal-branding/280371

Part 2: Why

- Simon Sinek, Start with Why
- https://hbr.org/2018/01/the-new-ceo-activists
- https://www.finn.agency/nl/communicatie-belgische-ceo-covid19/

- https://www.gsb.stanford.edu/sites/default/files/publication-pdf/cgri-closer-look-74-double-edged-sword-ceo-activism.pdf
- https://www.sdworx.be/nl-be/over-sd-worx/pers/2022-08-25-65-van-de-belgische-werkgevers-heeft-moeite-om-werknemers-aan-te
- Edelman Trust Barometer 2020
- Edelman Trust Barometer 2022
- Brunswick, Digital Investor Survey 2023
- The Double-Edged Sword of CEO activism, By David F. Larcker, Stephen A. Miles, Brian Tayan, and Kim Wright-Violich November 8, 2018 Stanford Closer Look series
- The Digital Reputation report, Propel, 2022
- https://www.britannica.com/topic/Renaissance-man
- https://www.museepicassoparis.fr/fr/la-collection
- https://nl.wikipedia.org/wiki/Volkslied_van_de_Europese_Unie
- https://www.science.org/doi/10.1126/science.aao0440
- Flux – author April Rinne

Part 3: Personal(ity)
- time.com/6293762/barbie-movie-ruth-handler/
- Barbie, 2023 (film)
- Oppenheimer, 2023 (film)
- www.yannarthusbertrandphoto.com
- Link, culture programme on Canvas 6 October 2000 - hetarchief.be
- Dare to Lead - Brené Brown
- Unfair Advantage - Carole Lamarque, published by LannooCampus
- Zoonotic - Carole Lamarque, published by LannooCampus
- Pretend It's a City - Martin Scorsese – Netflix

Part 4: Storytelling
- Crying CEO https://www.cnbc.com/2022/08/11/ceo-posts-crying-selfie-on-linkedin-after-laying-off-employees-and-it-goes-viral-.html
- https://www.ewi-vlaanderen.be/nieuws/met-falen-en-opstaan
- fuckupnights.com

Part 5: The Process
- Ruben Mersch, Van Mening Verschillen
- Ruben Mersch, Waarom iedereen altijd gelijk heeft
- Ruben Mersch podcast episode www.bravenewhuman.com
- https://www.goodmorningamerica.com/living/story/womans-linkedin-headshot-viral-message-work-life-balance-73195492
- https://www.gsb.stanford.edu/insights/what-separates-hitmakers-one-hit-wonders
- https://www.entrepreneur.com/science-technology/3-ways-to-become-an-overnight-success/377179

- www.ynharari.com/
- www.ted.com/talks/brene_brown_the_power_of_vulnerability
- https://www.youtube.com/watch?v=fgP2odkKhu4&ab_channel=MikhailaPeterson
- https://www.jordanbpeterson.com/about/
- https://prowsechowne.com/focus-understanding-controversy-surrounds-bill-c-16/
- I'm not your guru, Tony Robbins - Netflix
- Brunswick, Connected Leadership report 2022
- Flywheel of Thought Leadership by LinkedIn & Edelman
- The visible expert study by Hinge Marketing, 2020
- Larie Young, Thought Leadership, Kogan Page, 2013
- Gary Vaynerchuck, https://garyvaynerchuk.com/the-garyvee-content-strategy-how-to-grow-and-distribute-your-brands-social-media-content/
- https://garyvaynerchuk.com/the-show-that-started-it-all/
- Raymond Queneau https://en.wikipedia.org/wiki/Hundred_Thousand_Billion_Poems
- https://fr.wikipedia.org/wiki/Raymond_Queneau
- GIGO in AI https://www.forbes.com/sites/forbestechcouncil/2023/03/31/uncovering-the-different-types-of-chatgpt-bias/
- https://www.forbes.com/sites/cognitiveworld/2019/03/07/the-achilles-heel-of-ai/
- https://www.nemokennislink.nl/publicaties/veel-problemen-met-ai-kunnen-we-niet-alleen-vanuit-de-techniek-oplossen/
- https://blogs.scientificamerican.com/information-culture/the-impact-of-ted-talks/
- https://nl.wikipedia.org/wiki/Garbage_in,_garbage_out
- https://www.researchgate.net/publication/323312753_Measuring_Personal_Branding_in_Social_Media_Towards_an_Influence_Indication_Score

Part 6: Own Your A.I.

- https://digitaltwininsider.com/2023/03/16/nike-metaverse/
- https://www.fortnite.com/news/high-digital-fashion-drops-into-fortnite-with-balenciaga
- https://www.coca-colacompany.com/media-center/coca-cola-to-offer-first-ever-nft-collectibles
- https://rltylive.medium.com/7-global-celebrities-who-talk-about-the-metaverse-88420c420f6c
- youtube.com/watch?v=MVYrJJNdrEg&ab_channel=LexFridman
- https://www.trendingtopics.eu/dangerous-openai-releases-voice-cloning-tool-in-super-election-year/
- https://techxplore.com/news/2024-05-openai-johansson-gaffe-voice-cloning.html

- https://techcrunch.com/2024/05/19/creative-artists-agency-veritone-ai-digital-cloning-actors/?guccounter=1&guce_referrer=aHR0cHM6Ly93d3cuZ29vZ2xlLmNvbS8&guce_referrer_sig=AQAAALwYNq_XBzhQIUtH-DZ0JYMpe79HCB2Bmokjgo9wGNLOuiO6uatmnZpFzLIc4ZppQYutTUkNEVGGl7bPHfw6woX-pMclz5J8uLNDQzt68KwiDxkza7W_GxB5rRtp1G2VMALvEb8r7AZFSBzhsPDONz3xkf2FJBlh7YoiQfhh3WXT
- https://www.linkedin.com/posts/chris-ume-31452b3b_were-honored-to-have-been-part-of-robert-activity-7213192607252787200-QxGK?utm_source=share&utm_medium=member_desktop
- https://struckcapital.com/deepfakes-and-blockchain/
- https://www.hollywoodreporter.com/movies/movie-news/metaphysic-pro-ai-anne-hathaway-octavia-spencer-tom-hanks-1235590707/
- https://www.itu.int/hub/2024/05/ai-watermarking-a-watershed-for-multimedia-authenticity/
- https://www.nbcnews.com/tech/tech-news/hollywood-actor-sag-aftra-ai-artificial-intelligence-strike-rcna94191
- https://eu.usatoday.com/story/entertainment/tv/2023/08/01/ai-and-hollywood-strikes-what-the-real-threat-is-to-actors-writers/70436618007/
- https://www.forbes.com/sites/johnkoetsier/2023/08/16/as-hollywood-strikes-96-of-entertainment-companies-are-boosting-generative-ai-spend/
- Chris Nolan about the 'Oppenheimer moment' https://youtu.be/xSalnOwb7Bg?si=X03BCNjl9dJSRBN5
- Harari about the Oppenheimer moment in Ai https://youtu.be/Bpy6X7kF7-s?si=A5p66nviHRm4f15B
- Jennifer Lopez & Virgin: www.virginvoyages.com/l/jenai
- Holy Herndon: www.hollyherndon.com/
- https://www.forbes.com/sites/cognitiveworld/2019/03/07/the-achilles-heel-of-ai/
- https://www.reuters.com/article/us-amazon-com-jobs-automation-insight-idUSKCN1MK08G
- Podcaster Lex Fridman in conversation with Mr Beast about his clone youtu.be/Z3_PwvvfxIU?si=hzibQwQnE23OPUvY